Ten out of ten! Whoever
ancient Israel would be s
Well, God did actually. A   ully
explained, clearly illustrated and comp   1 of
one of the most famous but most forgotten chapters of the bible.
We ignore the commandments ('Christians aren't under law, but
under grace'), are scared of them ('Christians disagree over how
they apply today') or feel we've grown out of them ('Great for
Sunday school lessons or children's story Bibles, but that's about it').
But the Ten Commandments timelessly reveal God's priorities for
his redeemed people. In such a short book, there is so much to
reflect on and pray through. I repeatedly found myself saying under
my breath 'Brilliant!', 'I really needed to hear that' and 'How I love
your law, O God!' Highly recommended.
Dave Gobbett, Lead Minister, Highfields Church, Cardiff, and
Word Alive trustee

Clearly argued, thoughtfully applied and relentlessly practical, this
book draws from a wide range of biblical material to enable us to
see the sharp relevance of the Ten Commandments for our lives
today. At the same time, it draws us back continually to the gospel,
bringing grace for our failures and hope in our continuing battles
with sin.
John Risbridger, Minister and Team Leader, Above Bar Church,
Southampton, and Chair of Keswick Ministries

We all think we know the meaning of the Ten Commandments,
but are not altogether sure how they apply today. Graham Beynon
has given us an excellent introduction to both their meaning and
application. Placing them in the wider frame of the Bible, he has
shown us their immediate relevance in a steady, calm, godly, yet
common-sense manner. Even if you don't agree with all his
conclusions (although I hope you will), you will be made to think
as you are faced with their transparent wisdom and the challenge
of implementing them in our complex twenty-first-century world.
Derek Tidball, author and speaker, and formerly a pastor and
Bible college principal

I love the way this book brings the Ten Commandments to life for today's world. Far from being a remote, historical set of religious rules, this volume by Graham Beynon showed me how these ancient principles are bang up to date and acutely relevant for my life. The helpful, explanatory style really opened up my understanding and sharpened my conscience. I also liked the way many of the chapter headings illuminate the positive Christian virtues that are embedded in the commandments. Instead of being predictable, somewhat negative or irrelevant, the Ten Commandments turned out to be dynamic, refreshingly positive and wide-ranging in their impact. *Paul Valler, author of* Get a Life

SURPR!SED BY THE COMMANDMENTS

SURPRISED BY THE COMMANDMENTS

DISCOVERING NEW DEPTH AND RICHNESS

GRAHAM BEYNON

ivp

INTER-VARSITY PRESS
36 Causton Street, London SW1P 4ST, England
Email: ivp@ivpbooks.com
Website: www.ivpbooks.com

© Graham Beynon, 2016

Graham Beynon has asserted his right under the Copyright, Designs and Patents Act 1988 to be identified as Author of this work. All rights reserved. No part of this publication may be reproduced, stored in a retrieval system, or transmitted, in any form or by any means, electronic, mechanical, photocopying, recording or otherwise, without the prior permission of the publisher or the Copyright Licensing Agency.

Unless otherwise indicated, Scripture quotations are taken from the Holy Bible, New International Version (Anglicized edition). Copyright © 1979, 1984, 2011 by Biblica (formerly International Bible Society). Used by permission of Hodder & Stoughton Publishers, an Hachette UK company. All rights reserved. 'NIV' is a registered trademark of Biblica (formerly International Bible Society). UK trademark number 1448790.

Scripture quotations marked NIV84 are taken from the Holy Bible, New International Version. Copyright © 1973, 1978, 1984 by International Bible Society. Used by permission of Hodder & Stoughton Publishers, a member of the Hachette UK Group. All rights reserved. 'NIV' is a registered trademark of International Bible Society. UK trademark number 1448790.

Scripture quotations marked ESV are taken from The Holy Bible, English Standard Version,® copyright © 2001 by Crossway Bibles, a publishing ministry of Good News Publishers. Used by permission. All rights reserved.

British Library Cataloguing-in-Publication Data
A catalogue record for this book is available from the British Library.

ISBN: 978–1–78359–440–5
eBook ISBN: 978–1–78359–500–6

Set in 12/15pt Dante
Typeset in Great Britain by CRB Associates, Potterhanworth, Lincolnshire
Printed in Great Britain by Ashford Colour Press Ltd, Gosport, Hampshire

Inter-Varsity Press publishes Christian books that are true to the Bible and that communicate the gospel, develop discipleship and strengthen the church for its mission in the world.

IVP originated within the Inter-Varsity Fellowship, now the Universities and Colleges Christian Fellowship, a student movement connecting Christian Unions in universities and colleges throughout Great Britain, and a member movement of the International Fellowship of Evangelical Students. Website: www.uccf.org.uk. That historic association is maintained, and all senior IVP staff and committee members subscribe to the UCCF Basis of Faith.

These sermons were preached at Grace Church, Cambridge, a church plant in north Cambridge. It has been a wonderful church to help start and lead, an enriching church to teach and care for, and a caring and supportive church to be part of. And it is to that congregation that this book is dedicated.

CONTENTS

PREFACE

'How about the Ten Commandments?' David said, and my heart fell slightly.

It was a meeting of our church leaders, and we were discussing what our next sermon series would cover. Suggestions were being thrown around. I didn't have a firm favourite at that stage and was happy to consider anything. Except the Ten Commandments.

I don't know exactly why my heart fell, but it was very revealing that it did. I think it was a combination of thinking of the Ten Commandments as *predictable*, *negative* and *irrelevant*.

First, I thought they were predictable, and as a result a bit boring. I thought we knew what they said, and so there would be little that was fresh and new. Second, I thought of them as negative – lots of 'You shall not . . .' As the main preacher at our church I am very aware that telling people what *not* to do all the time gets a bit gloomy. Third, I thought they weren't very relevant. Not that I thought they were unimportant; of course we should worship only God and not make idols. Of course murder and stealing were wrong. But those weren't a great danger for most of us, and so I assumed that the appli-cation of these commands would feel a long way from people's lives. So a predictable, negative and irrelevant sermon series – no thanks, I wasn't keen.

But eventually that was the decision. And I am so glad it was.

As it turned out, it was one of the most enjoyable sermon series I have ever preached, and not only that, but one of the most talked about at our church. Rather than a feeling of predictability, there was a sense of discovery. In some cases, the commandments didn't say what we had assumed, or there was a depth and richness to them that we hadn't appreciated. And while they are indeed mainly framed negatively ('You shall not . . .'), we saw that they are wonderfully positive about how we can and should live. And rather than being irrelevant, we discovered a wealth of application into our daily lives. Discussions about what they mean for how we live today carried on in our small groups and were some of the most applied ones we've had.

For me, and for the church, there was the sense of *rediscovering* the Ten Commandments, and so coming to appreciate and value them afresh. My prayer is that the same will be true for you as you read this book.

ACKNOWLEDGMENTS

My thanks go to my editor Eleanor Trotter, who both encouraged this book into being and sharpened its final form. Also to Ed Moll, whose comments on a draft helped improve a number of sections.

INTRODUCTION
APPROACHING THE TEN COMMANDMENTS

I expect you know how word association games work. Someone says a word, and you say whatever comes to mind. So if I say 'cat', you probably say 'dog'.

What about if I say 'law'? What would you say then?

The associations tend to be negative: obedience, police, stop, enforcement, prison, command. 'Law' gives off the unmistakable smell of restriction and limitation.

That's true for laws in general, and probably even more so for religious laws and commands. People outside the church easily think of Christians as those who want to give them laws to follow so that they can impose their views on them. If they have a concept of God, he may well be someone who lays down the law and demands obedience to it. God and law can make for an unappealing cocktail. Such negative associations easily carry over to Christians as well – 'law' has bad PR even in the church.

So here's a surprising thought: *God's law is a good thing.*

God's laws show us the right way, the best way, and the most loving way to live. That means that the Ten Commandments are good laws for life. Laws that guide us in how to live life, and laws that are thoroughly life giving. That's the surprising thought we're going to explore.

The Ten Commandments today

The Ten Commandments used to be held in high esteem in society. At one point they formed the basis of many laws of the land. Today, however, only two of the ten remain on the statute book – murder and theft. The others have been seen to be unnecessarily restricting. If you tell people you're reading a book on the Ten Commandments, they'll probably look at you with an expression that says, 'Why on earth would you want to do that?'

Although people are negative about law, they can be positive about a moral code. So much so that some have come up with new versions of the Ten Commandments for today. The philosopher A. C. Grayling put together a secular Bible called *The Good Book*,[1] which includes his new ten commandments.

1. Love well.
2. Seek the good in all things.
3. Harm no others.
4. Think for yourself.
5. Take responsibility.
6. Respect nature.
7. Do your utmost.
8. Be informed.
9. Be kind.
10. Be courageous.

Notice that apart from number three there are no lines you might cross. The 'law' not to harm anyone else has become the only moral boundary today. Apart from that, it's freedom everywhere.

This rewriting of the Ten Commandments, and others like it, suggests that the laws in the Bible are restrictive and limiting, or at least outdated and irrelevant, whereas the new lists are suitable for life in the twenty-first century. And Christians can easily believe that themselves.

There can be a degree of biblical support for this negative view of law. The Ten Commandments come in the Old Testament as part of what is called the 'old covenant', which is the way God set up his relationship with his people, Israel. But in the New Testament there is a new covenant, a new relationship with God. And that new covenant speaks of how Jesus has brought an end to the law, and about being free from the law. So we can think the law really is out date, even for God.

Law in the Bible needs a new image! We need to rediscover what is so positive and affirming about God giving us laws in the first place. We need to embrace the idea of law as a good thing for us, rather than a negative thing against us. And we need to understand how law fits into the new covenant for Christians today. Then we'll be ready to study each of the commandments in detail in the chapters that follow.

The law doesn't make us God's people

Let's look at the setting for the Ten Commandments in Exodus 19. Here's how it starts:

> On the first day of the third month after the Israelites left Egypt – on that very day – they came to the Desert of Sinai. After they set out from Rephidim, they entered the Desert of Sinai, and Israel camped there in the desert in front of the mountain. (Exodus 19:1–2)

God has rescued his people from slavery in Egypt. He has then led them through the desert and brought them to Mount Sinai. God calls Moses up to the mountain and reminds them what he has done for them:

> Then Moses went up to God, and the LORD called to him from the mountain and said, 'This is what you are to say to the descendants of Jacob and what you are to tell the people of Israel: "You yourselves have seen what I did to Egypt, and how I carried you on eagles' wings and brought you to myself."'
> (Exodus 19:3–4)

God's people had been slaves in Egypt, oppressed and imprisoned. But God brought judgment on Egypt through a series of plagues, the last of which brought their freedom. Then God rescued them through the Red Sea and destroyed Pharaoh and his army. That is what God is referring to when he says, 'You yourselves have seen what I did to Egypt.'

Having rescued them from slavery, God has drawn them to him like a bird carrying its young home: 'I carried you on eagles' wings and brought you to myself.'

So God has carried this group out of Egypt, across the Red Sea, through the desert. And where has he brought them? To himself. The rescue from slavery wasn't simply so that they could be free. It was so that they could be free to come to him. God liberated them from oppression under Pharaoh so they could come into a new relationship with him as their Lord and their God.

Rescue by God is so that there can be relationship with God.

That was true for Israel and that is also true for Christians today. We're told in the New Testament that God has brought us out of the kingdom of darkness, he has rescued us from the slavery of sin and Satan, so that he can bring us to himself (see Galatians 4:4–6; Colossians 1:13–14).

So the first thing for us to see is that salvation comes *before* the giving of the law. God doesn't say, 'If you obey me, I will rescue you.' He says, 'I've rescued you, so now obey me.' This is why there is a 'preface' to the Ten Commandments themselves:

> And God spoke all these words:
>> 'I am the Lord your God, who brought you out of Egypt,
>> out of the land of slavery.'
> (Exodus 20:1–2)

Obeying God's law is not how they become God's people; it is how they should live because they are God's people.

Think of the analogy of adoption. Various friends of ours have adopted children. When their new child comes home, they will begin to tell them the 'family rules': how they do things in their house, how they need to listen to them as parents, to be kind to their new brothers and sisters, not watch TV all day, and so on.

But following the family rules isn't how the children become part of the family; it's how they should live because they are part of the family. So for God's people, obeying his law is how we should live because we are his people.

God goes on to speak about his people's privileged position and what that means for how they live:

> 'Now if you obey me fully and keep my covenant, then out of all nations you will be my treasured possession. Although the whole earth is mine, you will be for me a kingdom of priests and a holy nation.' These are the words you are to speak to the Israelites.
> (Exodus 19:5–6)

It sounds like they will only be this 'treasured possession' if they obey him. That's true, but we need to clarify what it is they have to do. The phrase 'obey me fully' is more literally 'listen to me': they need to hear what God says, the terms of the relationship, and keep their part of the bargain. That is keeping his 'covenant'.

A covenant is like a mixture of a contract and a promise. It's a bit like in a marriage when a couple make their vows – they are entering into a marriage covenant together. That covenant defines the shape of the relationship.

So to stay in relationship with God, they must keep God's covenant.

But that covenant included what they should do when they broke one of God's laws. So if an Israelite knew he had lied, he wasn't automatically out of the covenant. No, he had to confess his sin and offer a sacrifice. If he did, then God promised he would forgive him.

So God wasn't asking for perfection; he was asking for loyalty. He was saying, 'I've brought you to myself, and you will remain my people as long as you don't turn away from me.'

It's a bit like saying to an adopted child, 'You will be our child, loved by us, just as long as you don't run away from home.' It's a condition, but keeping it doesn't earn a place in the family.

So if Israel stays loyal, then God says that they will be his 'treasured possession'.

It's a lovely picture of something personal and prized. When our children were younger, we once did a photo shoot with them. The photographer suggested that each of them bring a favourite possession that might be included. So my daughter took her teddy bear, one son his favourite dinosaur, and the other son the blanket he carried everywhere. These were their prized possessions. God would have taken his people, as they are his treasured possession.

That's the privileged position that Israel had, and that privilege is now true of Christians. Peter says of those who trust in Jesus:

> But you are a chosen people, a royal priesthood, a holy nation, God's special possession, that you may declare the praises of him who called you out of darkness into his wonderful light. Once you were not a people, but now you are the people of God; once you had not received mercy, but now you have received mercy.
> (1 Peter 2:9–10)

This is Exodus 19 applied to Christians today. Those who believe in Jesus are now God's special possession, by his mercy.

So for Israel then, and for Christians now, *the law doesn't make us God's people.*

That is simple but crucial. If you're not a Christian, please understand this. This book is focusing on God's law, how he tells us to live. But obeying the law is not how you become a Christian; it's not what gets you right with God. As the apostle Paul says, 'We . . . know that a person is not justified by the works of the law, but by faith in Jesus Christ' (Galatians 2:15–16).

So we are not justified – made right with God – through obeying the law, but only through faith in Jesus and his perfect life for us and his death in our place.

There is actually a real danger in studying the Ten Commandments if we don't remember this truth. Each chapter might make you feel guilty or smug, depending on how you think you're doing in obeying it. But if we feel either of those responses, that reveals we think that our standing with God turns on our performance.

But we cannot climb any ladders of acceptance with God by our obedience, and we don't slide down the ladder through our failures either. Rather, we are placed at the top of the ladder by God because of Jesus and his perfect obedience on our behalf. The law doesn't make us God's people; Jesus does.

The law does show us how to live as God's people

God brings the Israelites into a relationship with him and then he tells them how they should live in that relationship: 'And God spoke all these words: "I am the LORD your God, who brought you out of Egypt, out of the land of slavery"' (Exodus 20:2).

And the next lines say, 'You shall . . .' and describe what sort of life they should lead.

God has rescued them, and now he explains the shape of their new relationship with him. In my adoption picture, he explains the family rules: this is how you are to live as my people.

We should see then not only that God's gracious rescue comes first, but that his laws come second, straight after it. God, as God, and God as their rescuer, has the right to tell them how to live.

The first set of those laws are the Ten Commandments in Exodus 20. They are clearly the 'stand-out' laws in a number of ways:

- they are given by God face to face with his people rather than through Moses (Deuteronomy 5:4);
- they are the first laws given, and are separated from the rest of the laws in Exodus and Numbers;
- they are written by the finger of God (Exodus 31:18), showing that these are God's primary laws for his people;

- they are written on stone rather than scroll (Exodus 31:18), emphasizing their permanence;
- they are placed in the ark of the covenant, showing their centrality to the covenant relationship (whereas other laws are placed beside the ark, Deuteronomy 10:5; 31:24–26).

The Ten Commandments are foundational for Israel in how they should live as God's people.

But then we get more detailed laws. For example, chapter 21 starts like this:

> These are the laws you are to set before them:
> If you buy a Hebrew servant, he is to serve you for six years. But in the seventh year, he shall go free, without paying anything.
> (Exodus 21:1–2)

The next chapters are full of this sort of detailed law. So it's helpful to distinguish between two sorts of law. There are *general* laws that remain true all the time – that is what we get in the Ten Commandments – although we'll have to think about how they apply today. Then there are *situational* laws which are specific to certain circumstances. They usually begin with the word 'If'.

So a general law says, 'Do not steal.' A situational law says, 'If [someone] steals an ox or a sheep and slaughters it or sells it . . .' (Exodus 22:1, NIV84).

The situational laws apply the general laws to specific situations and say what should happen. They take account of different motivations, extenuating circumstances, accidents and so on. So we know we should not murder (general law). But what happens if you are chopping wood and the axe head flies off and kills someone? See Exodus 21:13 and then Deuteronomy 19:5–6 and you'll find out.

So the Ten Commandments are like the main headings, and the situational laws are lots of worked examples. Or the Ten Commandments are like signposts, and the situational laws are a series of examples you find on your route. We can picture this in a diagram (see below): each general law results in a variety of situational laws.

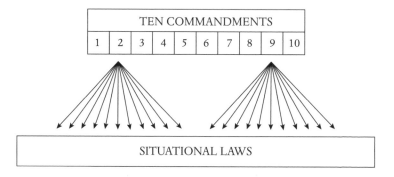

This difference between general and situational laws will be important for our study later on – we can explore the meaning of each commandment by looking at the worked examples. For now, though, the main point is that God's laws guided all of life for his people in the Old Testament. They told them about their legal system, their religious worship, family life and everything else.

This shows us two things. First, God is concerned for how his people live. He wants them to reflect his character, his truth and his holiness, in all their life. There is no part of life that becomes 'law-free' for God's people in the Old Testament.

Second, it also shows that the Ten Commandments aren't as simple as we might think. 'Do not steal' sounds pretty straightforward. But what about if you borrow a plough and it breaks while you're using it? Is that stealing? While the principles contained in the Ten Commandments are clear, the detailed, situational laws show that working them out in real life takes some thought.

But does the law really show Christians how to live today?

The law back then guided God's people in how to live. But what about God's people today?

I believe that the law does apply to Christians today, but does so differently from under the old covenant. We can see this in a couple of ways.

First, the law applies directly to Israel living in the situation of the Promised Land of Israel. They were a nation state living at a specific time, and many laws simply cannot be applied directly to life today (for example in our legal system).

Second, the law was part of the 'old covenant' relationship with God's people, but Christians are under a new covenant. The differences between the two are a source of great debate. But a key element is that Christians are not 'under' the law in the same way. Consider these verses:

> Before the coming of this faith, we were held in custody under
> the law, locked up until the faith that was to come would be
> revealed. So the law was our guardian until Christ came that
> we might be justified by faith.
> (Galatians 3:23–24)

The law here is like a temporary guardian that keeps people in check until Jesus comes. But with Jesus a new age starts where the law doesn't have the same role to play. Similarly, the Christian is spoken of as not being 'under the law' any more (see Galatians 5:18) and having 'died to the law' (Romans 7:4).

In the old covenant, people's relationship with God was 'under the law': it guided their life and determined their relationship with God. There were blessings and curses linked with their obedience to the law (see Deuteronomy 28). This led to God's discipline of his people and their eventual exile from the land for disobedience.

But now Jesus has taken the curse of the law on our behalf (Galatians 3:13). He is the culmination or the goal of the law (Romans 10:4). So Christians are not under the law like Old Testament believers were.

But the law is still relevant to believers today.

Jesus and the law

To see that relevance, let's look at some comments of Jesus on the law. He says, 'Do not think that I have come to abolish the Law or the Prophets; I have not come to abolish them but to fulfil them' (Matthew 5:17).

Jesus has come to fulfil rather than do away with the law. He goes on to quote some of the commandments and apply them to our motives. So rather than just not murdering, Jesus tells us not to be angry. Or rather than not committing adultery, Jesus tells us not to look lustfully (Matthew 5:21–22, 27–28). So Jesus thinks these commands still guide our behaviour today, and he applies them more fully, or shows their true intention.

We also see Jesus quoting the Ten Commandments as still applying to Christians. He says,

> But the things that come out of a person's mouth come from the heart, and these defile them. For out of the heart come evil thoughts – murder, adultery, sexual immorality, theft, false testimony, slander. (Matthew 15:18–19)

Jesus' point is that sin comes from out of our hearts. But look at his list of sins:

- murder (sixth commandment)
- adultery (seventh commandment) – expanded to include sexual immorality generally
- theft (eighth commandment)
- false testimony (ninth commandment) – expanded to include slander.

This list comes after Jesus has been arguing about obeying the command to honour your father and mother (fifth commandment).

So Jesus uses the Ten Commandments, along with some expansions, as his standards for living today. If we read passages on Christian living such as Ephesians 4 – 6 or Colossians 3, then we find a repetition of many of the Ten Commandments, and further expansion to cover related sins.

All this means that while our relationship with the law is different from that in the Old Testament, the Ten Commandments still show us how to live as God's people today.

The law shows us how to love as God's people

We see the guidance the law gives us today in a second way: it shows us how to love.

When Jesus is asked what the most important commandment is, this is how he replies:

> 'The most important one,' answered Jesus, 'is this: "Hear,
> O Israel: the Lord our God, the Lord is one. Love the Lord
> your God with all your heart and with all your soul and with
> all your mind and with all your strength." The second is this:

"Love your neighbour as yourself." There is no commandment greater than these.'
(Mark 12:29–31)

So all the law can be summed up under two headings: love God and love people. Christians are still to love God and love one another, and so the Ten Commandments show us something of what that means in practice.

So loving God will mean not having any other gods besides him (first commandment). Loving people will mean not stealing from them (eighth commandment). And so on for all the various laws. So we can add to our diagram (see below): we saw that the Ten Commandments are the main headings of God's law, expanded in the detailed laws that follow. But we can sum them all up with the command to love God and people.

This reinforces what we've seen above: the law helps us know how to live as God's people. But it adds something very important: it tells us that the law and love go together. In fact, the *law shows us how to love*.

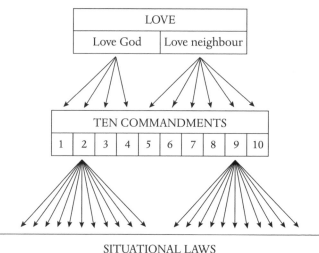

The apostle Paul says the same thing:

> The commandments, 'You shall not commit adultery,' 'You shall not murder,' 'You shall not steal,' 'You shall not covet,' and whatever other command there may be, are summed up in this one command: 'Love your neighbour as yourself.' Love does no harm to a neighbour. Therefore love is the fulfilment of the law.
> (Romans 13:9–10)

Paul says that all the laws are examples of love.

Today people tend to be positive about love and negative about laws. We all think we should love one another. But what does love look like in practice?

- Might it mean telling a small lie so that I don't hurt my friend's feelings? It's because I love her.
- Might it mean sleeping with my boyfriend? It's expressing my love for him.
- Could it mean borrowing the company car for the weekend holiday? It's a way of showing love to my family.

You see, we don't actually know what love looks like in practice. Today love is defined in positive ways that are very vague ('Do what's good for them'), or in negative ways that are very limited ('Don't hurt anyone'). But we need to know what love looks like up close and in detail.

So here's a different, more positive way to think about the law in general, and the Ten Commandments in particular: *they teach us how to love better.* In reading these next chapters, you should be finding out what it means to love God and one another in more detail.

The law makes us distinctive as God's people

We read these words from Exodus 19 earlier: ' "Although the whole earth is mine, you will be for me a kingdom of priests and a holy nation." These are the words you are to speak to the Israelites' (Exodus 19:5–6).

First, God's people were going to be 'priests'. Priests are people with a special relationship with God; they can approach him on behalf of other people. So here God says you will be a whole kingdom of priests. You will have a special status compared to other nations.

Second, they will be a 'holy nation'. Holiness is about being set apart for a special use. So God is saying, as a nation you are to be different from the nations around you.

As Israel lived differently in the world, people should notice. There are some verses in Deuteronomy on this:

> See, I have taught you decrees and laws as the LORD my God commanded me, so that you may follow them in the land you are entering to take possession of it. Observe them carefully, for this will show your wisdom and understanding to the nations, who will hear about all these decrees and say, 'Surely this great nation is a wise and understanding people.' What other nation is so great as to have their gods near them the way the LORD our God is near us whenever we pray to him? And what other nation is so great as to have such righteous decrees and laws as this body of laws I am setting before you today?
> (Deuteronomy 4:5–8)

See the idea? People will look at them and be impressed by how they live.

That is, they will be impressed if they are living by his laws.

They should be obeying God's laws because they should be obeying God; they should obey them because his laws are good for them, but they should also obey them for the sake of the rest of the world.

The same is to be true for Christians. As we live obeying God, we will live differently, and we will stand out in the world.

So Peter says,

Dear friends, I urge you, as foreigners and exiles, to abstain from sinful desires, which wage war against your soul. Live such good lives among the pagans that, though they accuse you of doing wrong, they may see your good deeds and glorify God on the day he visits us. (1 Peter 2:11–12)

For you have spent enough time in the past doing what pagans choose to do – living in debauchery, lust, drunkenness, orgies, carousing and detestable idolatry. They are surprised that you do not join them in their reckless, wild living, and they heap abuse on you. (1 Peter 4:3–4)

God's people are to be distinctive. Some people will mock us for that, but overall people will be drawn to it, as there is something wonderfully attractive about it. And our distinct life is part of our witness to the world.

So as we look through the Ten Commandments, we're going to think how we live differently in our society today, how we should stand out. And that's part of how we will draw others to God.

The law is a good thing

So we need to return to our surprising thought: God's law is a good thing.

Actually it's not surprising at all; it's biblical. Moses calls Israel to obey God's commands and says they are to 'observe the LORD's commands and decrees that I am giving you today for your own good' (Deuteronomy 10:13).

See the last phrase? God's commands are given for our good.

The apostle Paul says, 'The commandment is holy, righteous and good' (Romans 7:12).

But this is a biblical thought we wrestle with today: 'law' has negative associations, not positive ones. But in the Bible the law is a good way to live; it's how we will love God and one another.

Consider this:

- If God made us, he *knows* what's good for us.
- If God rescued us, he *wants* what's good for us.

Put those together and consider: what laws would God give his people? Negative, harsh, restrictive laws that suck all the fun out of life? Or positive, wholesome, life-giving, life-guarding laws that lead us in the best way to live?

Imagine walking where you know there are dangerous bogs or cliff edges, and how glad you would be of a fence that keeps you on safe ground. So think of God's law as that fence which keeps us safe from the damage we can easily cause one another and ourselves. Think of each separate commandment as another plank in that fence keeping you safe.

Or think of the law as being like rails for a train. In one sense they restrict its movement, but they are what make it able to run as it was designed – they are good for it. Or think of God's law as like the string for a kite. It holds it firmly, but in so doing, lets it fly as it should.

Rightly understood, we should be able to say, 'Thank you for this law; it is good for me.'

When the Reformer John Calvin had to design a new church service for his congregation, he wanted to include the Ten Commandments. But how do you make them part of a church service? First of all, *where* do you put them in a service? He placed them *after* confession and reassurance of forgiveness. That showed they were part of the believer's response in living for God, not how they gained merit with God. Second, *how* do you recite them? Rather than reading the commandments, he had the congregation *sing* them! That showed they were good commands that were to be prized and celebrated.

God's law is a right thing, a good thing, and a wonderful thing that we can obey. These are laws for life! That's what we want to rediscover in this book.

I pray that you will be surprised by the commandments and find depth and richness in them.

1. EXCLUSIVE LOYALTY

Question: 'George, will you take Alice to be your wife? Will you love her, comfort her, honour and cherish her, and, forsaking all others, be faithful to her as long as you both shall live?'

George: 'I will.'

I ask that question of people like George, and then Alice, whenever I conduct a wedding. I'm asking if they will accept the responsibilities of marriage in committing to love and care for their spouse. Most of the questions and statements in the wedding vows are framed positively: will you love, comfort and cherish?

But did you spot the negative element in there?

'Forsaking all others'. That raises the thought that there might be someone who could grab our affections instead, that there could be competition for our loyalty. And so we include a promise never to allow someone else to come above our spouse or prevent us from loving him or her as we should.

It's already there in the positive vows of loving and being faithful, but stating the negative makes the positive even clearer: 'I promise my love to you, above anyone else.' It turns a promise of love and faithfulness into a promise of *exclusive loyalty*.

It is that sort of promise that starts off the Ten Commandments:

> And God spoke all these words:
>   'I am the LORD your God, who brought you out of Egypt, out of the land of slavery.
>   'You shall have no other gods before me.'
> (Exodus 20:1–3)

God has rescued his people from slavery in Egypt and brought them to himself, and now he is telling them how to live as his rescued people. As we saw in the Introduction, Christians read this in the light of the rescue God has brought through Jesus. We can read, 'I am the Lord who brought you out of the realm of sin and death, through the death of my Son.' And then he says, 'You shall have no other gods before me.'

We're called to exclusive loyalty

The first part of our response to God is the promise to stay faithful to him and so, just like in marriage, to forsake all others. Unlike marriage, this call to exclusivity is because of what God has done: he is the God who has rescued us, so we are to have no other gods before him. He is the only one who has saved us, so he is to be the only God we have.

When it says, 'no other gods before me', the last part of the phrase is somewhat debated. It is literally no other gods 'in front of my face', or 'in my presence'. That might mean no other gods 'in front of me', or 'instead of me', or 'alongside me', or 'over against me'. But all these point to the same thing: there should be no other gods than me, no competing loyalties. I am your God and you must forsake all others.

This raises the question of other gods in the Bible. There are two ways that it speaks about this. First, it is very clear that the God spoken of here is the only true God, the one who created the world, the one behind everything and who rules everything. In that sense there are no other gods. God says it himself: 'I am God, and there is no other' (Isaiah 45:22).

But, second, the Bible recognizes that people do worship other gods. It says that these are make-believe gods, nothing in themselves. But they can be something to some people, and they can be seen as real to us. So Jeremiah talks about idols that people worship, but also says, 'they are not gods at all' (Jeremiah 2:11).

In the New Testament, Paul says that 'An idol is nothing at all in the world' and that 'There is no God but one.' But he goes on to say that they are 'so-called gods' that people still worship (1 Corinthians 8:4–6).

This was seen in the nations around Israel where lots of different gods were worshipped. Some of the most famous were Baal, Ashtoreth and Molech. They were often thought of as having their own areas of expertise: one was the god of weather, while another specialized in fertility, and so on.

So God's people were told that such gods are only fakes. But there was also a realistic understanding that they might be drawn to them. God's people could think, 'We worship the Lord, but the harvest isn't doing so well and I've heard about this other god the nations worshipped who is god of the harvests, so maybe I'll offer a sacrifice to him as well.'

They faced the temptation to two-time God, to look elsewhere for blessing and help, or in the worst case, the temptation to abandon God and follow one of these other gods altogether. And so God says, 'You are to have no other gods before me.' Just as faithfulness in marriage means saying 'No' to anyone else who might ensnare our affections, so faithfulness to God involves saying 'No' to anything we would treat as a 'god'.

Remember, the Ten Commandments help us know what it means to love God. The first part of loving God properly is having no rivals to him, not flirting with other gods, and remaining completely loyal to him.

Loyalty in practice

This command to exclusive loyalty is unpacked through the rest of the law and later on in the Old Testament. First, there are repeated warnings not to follow the gods of these nations around them. Here are some examples:

> Whoever sacrifices to any god other than the Lord must be destroyed.
> (Exodus 22:20)

> Do not invoke the names of other gods; do not let them be heard on your lips.
> (Exodus 23:13)

> Do not follow other gods, the gods of the peoples around you.
> (Deuteronomy 6:14)

> You shall have no foreign god among you;
>   you shall not worship any god other than me.
> I am the Lord your God,
>   who brought you up out of Egypt.
> (Psalm 81:9–10)

Do you see how those drum in the same idea? Don't turn to, call on or worship any other god. God calls us to total, exclusive loyalty.

This means that God has severe words for anyone in Israel who teaches anyone to have other gods beside him. He says,

> If a prophet, or one who foretells by dreams, appears among you and announces to you a sign or wonder, and if the sign or wonder spoken of takes place, and the prophet says, 'Let us follow other gods' (gods you have not known) 'and let us worship them,' you must not listen to the words of that prophet or dreamer.
> (Deuteronomy 13:1–3)

Even if someone seems to be from God because he or she can tell the future, if the person tells you to worship another god, you must not listen to him or her. In fact, shocking as it might seem to us, the individual must be killed.

It goes on to say that the same treatment must apply, no matter who the person is:

> If your very own brother, or your son or daughter, or the wife you love, or your closest friend secretly entices you, saying, 'Let us go and worship other gods' (gods that neither you nor your ancestors have known, gods of the peoples around you, whether near or far, from one end of the land to the other), do not yield to them or listen to them. Show them no pity. Do not spare them or shield them. You must certainly put them to death. Your hand must be the first in putting them to death, and then the hands of all the people. Stone them to death, because they tried to turn you away from the LORD your God, who brought you out of Egypt, out of the land of slavery. Then all Israel will hear and be afraid, and no one among you will do such an evil thing again.
> (Deuteronomy 13:6–11)

This shows us what an evil thing it is to turn away from the true God, the one who saved them.

This also results in how God speaks and acts when his people do turn to other gods. So in Jeremiah 2 God laments over how Israel has turned away from him to follow other gods:

This is what the Lord says:
'I remember the devotion of your youth,
    how as a bride you loved me
and followed me through the wilderness,
    through a land not sown . . .
This is what the Lord says:
'What fault did your ancestors find in me,
    that they strayed so far from me?
They followed worthless idols
    and became worthless themselves.
They did not ask, 'Where is the Lord,
    who brought us up out of Egypt
and led us through the barren wilderness,
    through a land of deserts and ravines,
a land of drought and utter darkness,
    a land where no one travels and no one lives?' . . .
The priests did not ask,
    'Where is the Lord?'
Those who deal with the law did not know me;
    the leaders rebelled against me.
The prophets prophesied by Baal,
    following worthless idols.
'Therefore I bring charges against you again,'
                            declares the Lord.
    'And I will bring charges against your children's
        children.

Cross over to the coasts of Cyprus and look,
>   send to Kedar and observe closely;
>   see if there has ever been anything like this:
has a nation ever changed its gods?
>   (Yet they are not gods at all.)
But my people have exchanged their glorious God
>   for worthless idols.
Be appalled at this, you heavens,
>   and shudder with great horror,'

>>>>   declares the LORD.

'My people have committed two sins:
They have forsaken me,
>   the spring of living water,
and have dug their own cisterns,
>   broken cisterns that cannot hold water.'
(Jeremiah 2:2–13)

Notice the charges: they have forsaken the true God and followed other gods instead; they have prophesied by Baal; they have exchanged their glorious God for worthless idols.

Notice the feel: God remembers their devotion in days gone by; he laments their unfaithfulness; he calls on creation to be appalled at what they've done.

Notice the stupidity: they've left the glorious true God for worthless idols; they've left the spring of living water for cisterns that cannot hold water at all.

Notice the result: God will bring charges against them.

It is this turning away from God, breaking the first commandment, that eventually results in Israel being punished through the exile from the Promised Land. Here's the explanation given:

All this took place because the Israelites had sinned against the
LORD their God, who had brought them up out of Egypt from
under the power of Pharaoh king of Egypt. They worshipped
other gods and followed the practices of the nations the LORD
had driven out before them, as well as the practices that the
kings of Israel had introduced . . . They set up sacred stones
and Asherah poles on every high hill and under every spreading
tree. At every high place they burned incense, as the nations
whom the LORD had driven out before them had done. They
did wicked things that aroused the LORD's anger. They
worshipped idols, though the LORD had said, 'You shall not
do this.'
(2 Kings 17:7–12)

Elsewhere this turning to other gods is called adultery against
God. It is as if God is the husband and Israel is his wife. He
has called her to faithfulness, to exclusive loyalty, to him, but
she commits adultery. So Hosea says,

'I will punish her for the days
      she burned incense to the Baals;
she decked herself with rings and jewellery,
      and went after her lovers,
      but me she forgot,'
                              declares the LORD.
(Hosea 2:13)

Think how you would feel if your husband or wife turned his
or her back on you and ran after other people. Imagine your
spouse dressing up to attract lovers, but ignoring you. It's
awful, isn't it? That's what Israel did and what we do when we
break the first commandment.

The demand for exclusive loyalty

It's worth asking the question: how do people feel today about this sort of demand for exclusive loyalty? What reactions might it provoke?

I think it brings a mixed reaction. In marriage, everyone thinks such devotion is lovely – at least on the wedding day. It's wonderful to make such promises. And people think it's lovely on a golden wedding anniversary as well: how wonderful – they've stuck with each other for so long.

But sometimes people say that such demands for exclusivity are excessive and unhealthy. Why shouldn't I have some freedom? Why can't I untie these knots for someone else?

We need to see that the exclusive demands are *part of the nature* of marriage – it is two people committing to each other. And so exclusivity then also *protects* what marriage is.

On my desk in front of me is a photo of my wife which reminds me of her and our relationship. But imagine that I had a picture of someone else next to her whom I was attracted to. Having that picture would not only be wrong, but it would be profoundly unhelpful and destructive to our marriage.

So it is with God. Exclusive loyalty is simply the nature of the relationship: he is our God and no one else is. But it is also for the good of the relationship and to protect it. In marriage, it is only within the committed exclusiveness that flourishing and growth can happen. Take away the exclusiveness and the whole thing is undermined.

Exclusive loyalty to God is for our good because it is the only way the relationship can work and grow.

So here's the point: God doesn't demand exclusive loyalty because he's insecure and needs our loyalty to affirm him. That loyalty is part of the nature of the relationship and how our relationship with him will flourish.

'You shall have no other gods before me.' That is both right and good for us.

Beware of all other gods

This means we need to beware of other gods. We must beware of following them, beware of turning to them, and beware of worshipping them.

For the Israelites, the other gods were obvious: the gods of the nations around them. That means in the first instance that we should not follow the gods of the other religions of the world.

It means you cannot be a Christian and a Hindu, or a Muslim, or a Buddhist, or anything else. It means you cannot be a Christian and say the odd prayer to Vishnu. God calls us to forsake all others.

It means we must never look to other sources than God for supernatural guidance or help. For God's people in the Old Testament, this meant never using sorcerers or mediums or anything similar (see Deuteronomy 18:9–14). To do so would be to approach such powers as God. Today that means shunning fortune-tellers, psychic mediums, Ouija boards and spiritualists. It means we don't read the horoscopes, or rather that we don't believe them or act on them (you can read them, but make sure you laugh at them).

It also means that Christians shouldn't be members of societies like Freemasons. Much of Freemasonry is about charitable work, but it has a religious basis, and its ceremonies involve praying to 'god' and making declarations about this 'god'. But this is not the God of the Bible. One friend who was involved with the Freemasons became a Christian and instinctively felt very uncomfortable. That was a good sign! It was like feeling uncomfortable about a close relationship with someone at work when you've got married – you know it might challenge the exclusive loyalty you should have.

Those are some first obvious applications. But what other challenges to exclusive loyalty are there? The commandment is about 'having' other gods. So we must ask what it means to 'have' a god. The Reformer Martin Luther pins this down:

> A god means that from which we are to expect all good and to which we are to take refuge in all distress, so that to have a God is nothing else than to trust and believe him from the whole heart . . . That now, I say, upon which you set your heart and put your trust is properly your god.[2]

The biggest challenge for most of us is with alternative 'functional gods'. Such a god is something that isn't religious (like the god of another religion), but it operates like a god in your life. So you look to it for help or blessing. You trust in it and what it will give you. You live for it and follow what it tells you.

Jesus gives us the example of money:

> No one can serve two masters. Either you will hate the one and love the other, or you will be devoted to the one and despise the other. You cannot serve both God and Money.
> (Matthew 6:24)

Jesus pictures God and money as two alternative masters you could live for. Money becomes a rival to the true God, because it can act like a functional god. Worshipping it doesn't involve setting up an altar in the lounge at home, but it does involve living for money, relying on money, loving money and trusting money.

But there are other functional gods than money. We're told of a variety of things we could love or worship instead of the true God. They include:

- possessions (Luke 12:16–21)
- pleasure (2 Timothy 3:4)
- food (Philippians 3:19)
- self (Daniel 4:30; 2 Timothy 3:2)
- our own power (Habakkuk 1:11).

We could go on. I could worship family, reputation, success, image, appearance, fashion, technology, music, popularity, and more. These become 'God-substitutes'.

It is of course all about my attitude to them. And that can be difficult to determine sometimes. Many of these are good things that we turn into 'god things'. So for any one of them, ask yourself:

- How do I feel about it?
- How would I feel if I didn't have it?
- What do I think it gives me?
- Why do I like it?

And pray, asking God to help you identify functional gods in your life.

This also means we must act if anyone tries to tempt us to follow other gods. Just as that person wasn't to be tolerated within Israel, the individual must not be allowed to teach in the church. This is why there are strong words about rejecting any false teachers in the New Testament (see 2 Peter 2).

Instead of temptation to unfaithfulness, what we want in our churches is encouragement to loyalty. We need to help one another see that God is the true God, he is the one who

has loved and saved us, and so he is the only God worth
having. And so we urge one another to stay faithful to him.

Responding to God

This command is at the very heart of what it means to be one
of God's people, for the heart of sin is that we do not worship
God, but worship something else instead. So Paul says,

> For although they knew God, they neither glorified him as God
> nor gave thanks to him, but their thinking became futile and their
> foolish hearts were darkened. Although they claimed to be wise,
> they became fools and exchanged the glory of the immortal God
> for images made to look like a mortal human being and birds and
> animals and reptiles.
> (Romans 1:21–23)

We all exchange the true and glorious God for a pathetic
substitute.

Then, at conversion, we recognize the wrongness of this
and turn from it. So Paul described the conversion of believers
in Thessalonica like this:

> They tell how you turned to God from idols to serve the living
> and true God, and to wait for his Son from heaven, whom he raised
> from the dead – Jesus, who rescues us from the coming wrath.
> (1 Thessalonians 1:9–10)

So in repentance and faith, we turn from what we worshipped
before and trust in the true God and his offer of salvation
in Jesus.

If only we could leave it there! But we can't, because we
then keep on breaking this command. Having turned around

in repentance, we keep on turning back to glance behind us. Having turned from our idols, we keep on trusting them – at least a bit. And so we need to keep on being told: 'You shall have no other gods before me.'

So we need to respond to this command in continuing repentance. That means identifying where we continue to break it and confessing that sin. That is one purpose of God's law: revealing our sin more clearly. So reflecting on this should pull us up short and make us see how we have disobeyed God. It may very well mean that we feel guilty, but there is a solution to guilt, and his name is Jesus.

Jesus was the one who always obeyed this command. He never followed any other god. He was tempted by Satan, who said, 'All this [the kingdoms of the world] I will give you . . . if you will bow down and worship me.' But Jesus replied, 'Away from me, Satan! For it is written: "Worship the Lord your God, and serve him only"' (Matthew 4:8–10).

Jesus always obeyed this command. He succeeded where we have failed. And then he swaps places with us, takes our punishment and gives us his righteousness. Remember from the Introduction: the law doesn't make us God's people. We are accepted only in Jesus.

So, as we are convicted about having other gods before God, we run to Jesus and we are glad and grateful for him.

But then we want to live out this command each day. The law also shows us how to live as God's people. We want to continue to repent, turning round and living differently. We want to respond in faith, believing this command is right and good. We want to show true love for God by exclusive loyalty to him.

We need to take these issues seriously. Putting my confidence in money or elsewhere doesn't *feel* that bad. So we have to tell ourselves that we're talking about spiritual adultery

– worse than physical adultery. We're talking about abandoning the God who created us and loved us. We're talking about following other gods, ones that haven't saved or loved us. Take money: what has money ever done for you? Has money cared for you, sacrificed for you or forgiven you? No. But the true God has.

Plus these false gods are gods that will ultimately betray us and let us down, which the true God never will do. The history of Israel is of people following other gods and discovering too late that they are useless and pathetic. We want to see that clearly and be warned.

So we want to turn from our idols. We want to fight against them, throw them out. We want to say to God, 'You are the only true God; you are the one who rescued me and loved me. Help me stay loyal to you alone.'

2. ACCEPTING WHO GOD IS

Have you heard the story about the woman who invented her own religion?

No, it's not a joke. Her name was Sheila Larson. She was interviewed as part of a religious survey, and that interview then appeared in a book. She had invented her very own personal religion. She said it was about trying to love yourself and be gentle with yourself. And she said it had really helped her.

As her name was Sheila, she called her religion 'Sheilaism'. (It really is true.) 'Sheilaism' has gone on to become a known term among sociologists who are referring to an individual private religion (you can find an entry on Wikipedia).

I guess that you find that pretty weird. After all, it is very odd to think you can make up your own religion.

But I want to suggest that it's not weird at all. It is in fact what most people do.

People pick a religion, but then decide which bits they like and which they want to discard. Or they choose different ideas about God and life and put them all together to form a picture of 'God' or whatever they want to call him or her or it. They decide on their view of the purpose of life and how we should live. They connect that with what they think is good and bad, right and wrong, and how to treat other people.

But in making all these choices, they are making up a religion.

You hear it most clearly when people say, 'I like to think of God as . . .', and they fill in the rest. And that is a common phrase today. It means everyone gets to decide what God is like. Everyone makes up their own religion.

When you think about it, the only weird thing about Sheila's religion is that she named it, and named it after herself. We don't do that because that *is* weird. But we do make up a picture of God that we ourselves like.

Which brings us to the second commandment:

> You shall not make for yourself an image in the form of anything in heaven above or on the earth beneath or in the waters below. You shall not bow down to them or worship them; for I, the LORD your God, am a jealous God, punishing the children for the sin of the parents to the third and fourth generation of those who hate me, but showing love to a thousand generations of those who love me and keep my commandments.
> (Exodus 20:4–6)

Idols or images?

This command is often misunderstood. We easily think of other religions that have physical idols: Hinduism, for example, has the elephant god Ganesh. And we assume God is saying, 'Don't have any idols like that; don't bow down to them or worship them.'

But if this is referring to idols from other religions, then that would make it a repeat of the first commandment: 'You shall have no other gods.' In fact, some traditions of interpretation put verses 3 and 4 together to make it two parts of the first commandment, precisely because they think it's saying the same thing again.

But most interpreters think it's a second and separate command, and I agree. The first command is *no other gods*; but the second is *no images of God*. Those images may be in the form of making idols, but they are images of the true God, rather than of other gods. God is saying, 'Do not make any images (of me) and do not bow down to them or worship them.'

The first command is saying that only God is to be worshipped. The second command is about *how* he is to be worshipped.

Beware of 'recreating' God

To put it differently, the warning is against 'recreating' God. Beware of picturing God as being like something else, in the form of something in creation. So God says: don't look at anything in the sky (whether birds or stars), or anything on the earth (whether animals or mountains), or anything in the sea (whether fish or whales), and say, I think God is like that. Do not use anything in creation to picture God.

We can see this more clearly when we look at how this command is repeated and expanded. Leviticus says,

> Do not make idols or set up an image or a sacred stone for yourselves, and do not place a carved stone in your land to bow down before it. I am the LORD your God.
>
> (Leviticus 26:1)

This is one of many examples that repeats the second commandment: do not make idols or images as an object of worship. This comes again and again as a warning throughout the law and later books. We often assume that these sorts of warnings are against adopting the idols of the other nations – and some of them are. But others are against creating any image, or idol, of the one true God.

We see this especially clearly in Deuteronomy where there is more of an explanation of the second commandment:

> You saw no form of any kind the day the LORD spoke to you at Horeb out of the fire. Therefore watch yourselves very carefully, so that you do not become corrupt and make for yourselves an idol, an image of any shape, whether formed like a man or a woman, or like any animal on earth or any bird that flies in the air, or like any creature that moves along the ground or any fish in the waters below.
> (Deuteronomy 4:15–18)

Do you see the repetition of the second commandment here? They are told: do not make for yourself any idol or image picked from any part of creation. But the reason is because God didn't appear in any visible form. The logic is this: God didn't show you what he looked like, so don't start drawing him. He didn't appear in a certain shape or form, so don't give him one.

We see an illustration of this later in the book of Exodus in an event relating to a golden calf. Moses is on the mountain talking with God. He is gone for a while, and so Aaron, his brother and assistant, makes a golden calf that the people start to worship (see Exodus 32).

But they weren't breaking the first commandment in worshipping a different god. Aaron said about the golden calf,

'These are your gods, Israel, who brought you up out of Egypt' (Exodus 32:4). He goes on to say that with this calf they will have a festival to the LORD – using the personal name for their God (Exodus 32:5). So the golden calf doesn't replace God (the first commandment), but it pictures God (the second commandment). You can see other examples later in Israel's history in Judges 17:3–4 and 1 Kings 12:28–29.

God is saying: don't recreate me to look like something else.

Why no images?

So why does God give this command? Why forbid images?

In Isaiah 40, God compares himself with idols that people make, and he asks,

> With whom, then, will you compare God?
>> To what image will you liken him?
> (Isaiah 40:18)

He goes on to talk about the idols made from wood and overlaid with gold. But God reigns over and above creation. And so he again asks,

> 'To whom will you compare me?
>> Or who is my equal?' says the Holy One.
> (Isaiah 40:25)

The point is that there is no adequate image for God in creation – not in the sky, or the earth, or the sea.

No image can capture God. Remember, God is the one who made all creation: what is in the heavens, the earth and the waters. Each thing he made tells us something about him, but it cannot be an adequate description of him. Anything picked from creation to depict God will picture less than God is and will distort who he is.

Imagine artists who paint pictures, or inventors who make machines. You could look at what they create and that would tell you something about them. But it cannot sum them up adequately. What they make is far less than what they are as individuals.

So it is with God. He is so much greater than his creation, so nothing in creation can adequately picture him. In fact, as soon as we use an image, we have reduced and reshaped God.

You may have been thinking though, doesn't the Bible itself describe God using terms from creation?

And the answer is 'Yes'. We are told that God is like a rock, which pictures his stability (Deuteronomy 32:4). He is like a strong tower, which pictures his protection (Psalm 61:3). He is like a consuming fire, which pictures his punishment (Hebrews 12:29). So examples from creation are indeed regularly used to help us know what God is like.

But we only know God is like these things because he has told us. He controls the picture. We don't look round creation and say, 'I think God is wobbly like a jellyfish.' He tells us what he is like and not like, and he uses terms from creation as metaphors or pictures, to help us understand.

Also, no one of those metaphors can sum God up. He is far more than any one of them, or even all of them combined. And so we should not take a rock or a tower or some fire, and use it to represent God. We must not bow down to it or worship it.

So it's not that God is against images as such, because he uses them himself. But he gets to choose the image; he tells us what it means, and tells us that he is far more than any single image.

We know God isn't against images, because he sent his Son Jesus who is described as the image of the invisible God (Colossians 1:15). When we look at Jesus, we see God. But we are told about Jesus in words. And Jesus cannot be summed up or represented by anything else in creation.

God has wonderfully taken the initiative to reveal himself to us. He has spoken to us and described himself in words so that we know what he is like. We don't get an exhaustive description; the Bible doesn't and can't tell us everything about God. But it does tell us true things about him. And the second commandment is saying, 'I've told you what I'm like, so don't picture me as something else.'

Do you see the issue at stake here? Who gets to define God – us or him? Remember Sheila Larson? She made up her own religion, with its own picture of God. And that is what everyone does when they say, 'I like to think of God as . . .' and fill in the blank. Making an image is such a big deal because it is distorting the true picture and changing the God we worship.

It is also profoundly insulting to God. God reveals himself to us, and then we say, 'I'd like to think of you like this instead.' It's like someone giving you a painting and then you decide to 'improve' it by painting over sections, adding or removing parts. How dare we 'improve' on God!

No images because God is 'jealous'

This leads us to the reason God gives us in Exodus 20:

> I, the LORD your God, am a jealous God, punishing the children
> for the sin of the parents to the third and fourth generation of
> those who hate me, but showing love to a thousand generations
> of those who love me and keep my commandments.
>
> (Exodus 20:5–6)

Our first problem here is that the word 'jealousy' is almost always used negatively today. It doesn't have any positive associations. And we all know too well that we can be jealous in an ugly, petty, mean sort of way.

So we need to push those thoughts out of our minds, because God's jealousy is not like that. This is like the right jealousy of a husband or a wife for his or her spouse. Each rightly wants the other's loyalty and affection. It might be better to translate it as being zealous or passionate.

We used the image of marriage in the last chapter. The first commandment of 'No other gods' is like saying to a wife, 'No other men'. Here the second command is more like saying, 'Don't try to change him.' Or don't wish him to be different from how he really is. That is a different sort of disloyalty, but it is still disloyalty. And while we might wish our spouses to be different because we're all flawed, we can never wish that of God.

So God is jealous. He is wonderfully loving, but he is not a wet, pushover, 'I don't mind how you think of me' sort of God.

This jealousy leads to God's punishment and blessing. Verse 5 can seem like it's saying that God punishes children for the sins of their parents, which doesn't sound very fair. And elsewhere God explicitly says that the innocent won't die for the sins of other people (Exodus 23:7; Deuteronomy 24:16; Ezekiel 18:19–20).

I don't think it means that later generations are punished for things which they haven't done. Rather, the three to four generations spoken of probably refers to a family group in existence at one time. There would have been three or four generations alive: parents, children, grandchildren, and sometimes great-grandchildren too.

The nature of family and society was that if the parents made changes in their worship, then the rest of the family followed suit. That is why it says the third or fourth generation of 'those who hate me'. The later generations are seen as hating God; they have followed their parents in this distortion of him.

Similarly, in verse 6 we're told that God's love will extend to a thousand generations of those who love him and keep his commandments. This is not saying that just as long as you have some godly ancestors you'll be fine. The Israelites didn't automatically reap the consequences of earlier generations. Rather, God's treatment of them depended on their own response.

The point here is twofold. First, you cannot mess around with God and expect to get away with it. He is a jealous God. He will not tolerate us changing him and reshaping him.

But second, his covenant promise of love far outweighs his punishment. It is three to four generations versus a thousand. God is saying that his covenant faithfulness and love will continue on and on. Those who respond to me as I truly am, those who respond in love to me – they will find that I am a consistent, constant, loving God who will never let them down.

What about visual arts?

This command has raised significant questions over the use of visual arts generally, but especially in churches. In the Protestant Reformation, questions were raised over 'icons' – pictures of Jesus or saints – which were used in the Roman Catholic Church. And questions were raised over stained-glass pictures in church buildings along with statues and crosses.

The concern was this: isn't all this visual art breaking the second commandment? Isn't it picturing God using something from creation? Indeed, this has meant that some church traditions have been against visual arts altogether, resulting in very plain church buildings: no stained glass, crosses or statues.

I think the issue is more complicated than that. I certainly don't think it means God is against art in general or even against art within the church. For example, in the tabernacle and temple in the Old Testament people were told to have a variety of images of plants and trees, cherubim and so on (see Exodus 25). Rich visual symbolism abounded there.

So God isn't against visual art itself. He's against art that tries to represent him and is used as a means of worshipping him.

Take stained-glass windows. They could picture teaching from the Bible, say a parable of Jesus. So you can look at it and be reminded of that parable. It could even be used as a teaching tool, explaining what is happening. That is what many parents do when reading story Bibles to their children, and I think that's fine. But if a stained-glass window had a picture of Jesus and you were encouraged to meditate on it or pray to it, then it has clearly become an object of worship.

We see an example of this in the Old Testament. In Numbers, God saved his people by the making of a bronze snake. As people looked at the snake (trusting God's promise of salvation), they would be healed from the bites of the actual snakes that were killing them (see Numbers 21:4–9). After the event the bronze snake was kept. Presumably, it reminded them of that incident and God's gracious forgiveness. But later we're told that some of the Israelites started burning incense to it.

There was nothing wrong with the object in and of itself, but now it was being treated as an object of worship. So what did King Hezekiah do? He broke it into pieces (2 Kings 18:4).

That was the right response. If any object, or totem, or picture, or cross, or anything else starts to becomes an object of worship, or a means of worship, we should get rid of it. Ask yourself this question: is there any physical object or visual image that I feel I need to have in order to be able to worship God? If we say 'Yes', then we might be in danger of breaking the second commandment.

Mental images of God

But more significant to many of us is not physical images of God, but our mental image of him. I don't mean what we think he looks like (because we don't know), but what we think he is like.

We mentioned that common phrase, 'I like to think of God as . . .'

This is common in our culture, but we hear it in the church as well. It is perfectly possible for us to reshape God. All we have to do is start emphasizing part of what he is like and ignoring the other things he says about himself, and before long we will have a distorted picture. We will say, 'This is what God is like; here is the God of the Bible', but God wouldn't recognize himself at all.

The fact is that this has been done time and time again throughout history. It usually involves cutting off talk of God's judgment or wrath, and emphasizing his love and care. But sometimes it's been the reverse, and God's grace has been lost. Sometimes it's been emphasizing his closeness to us and losing his sovereignty over us, but again sometimes it's been the opposite and God has become distant and remote.

This is about having a balanced, biblical view of God, a view that takes everything he says about himself seriously. But more than that, it is about having a heart that is willing to listen to God and accept him for who he says he is, rather than trying to remould him.

He is no mouldable, plastic God. We can't change him and say we'd prefer him to be like this.

I remember being in Paris and seeing some wonderful statues in a park. Just imagine if I had got my hammer and chisel out of my bag and started hammering away, changing the sculpture. And if someone had asked what I thought I was doing, I'd replied, 'I'd prefer it to look different.'

That is what we are doing when we create images of God. And God won't have it. He has told us who he is, what he's like, and won't have us knocking bits off here and adding bits on there.

God has revealed himself to us. The question is: do we listen to what he says, or do we recreate him as we'd like him to be?

Responding to God

Consider ways in which you have broken, and continue to break, this command. Ways in which you are tempted to reshape God, and the times when you have given in to that temptation. Confess your sin now.

Realize how serious this is. Ask for his forgiveness.

Celebrate Jesus, who never made an image of God, either physical or mental. He knew him and trusted him for who he was. He never broke this commandment. And he did this all for us.

Then ask God to help you obey. Identify the areas where you are tempted, the places where you want to think of God differently from how he's revealed himself. Guard yourself in these, watch your thoughts, and ask for God's help to embrace him as he truly is.

3. HONOURING GOD RIGHTLY

The *Antiques Roadshow* is not a TV programme that I watch – I feel a need to make that clear – but I do understand the appeal. What people want is to be told that their jumble sale junk is actually a valuable antique. The biggest find on the show at the time of writing is a painting bought for £400 that turned out to be worth £400,000. I guess one of the motivations for watching is seeing people make that type of discovery (or being very disappointed).

Imagine you've had that sort of moment: something that has been sitting in the back of the garage for years turns out to be very precious. You'd find yourself saying, 'I didn't realize how valuable it was.' You hold it more carefully now. You certainty wouldn't put it back in the garage now.

The point is this: how valuable something is changes the way we treat it.

And that is the principle behind the third commandment: 'You shall not misuse the name of the LORD your God, for the

LORD will not hold anyone guiltless who misuses his name'
(Exodus 20:7).

We need to think about two things: what is the importance
of God's name, and what does it mean to misuse it?

The Lord's name

Names aren't as important to us today as they were in Bible
times. But even today we can be aware of the significance of
someone's name. In the case of false accusation, someone
might say, 'I want to clear my name.' Or we'll speak of
someone's achievements and say, 'They've made a name for
themselves.' So someone's name can sum up who the person
is and what he or she has done.

The same is true of God's name, except even more so,
because God chooses a special name to sum himself up.

The Lord's name here does not simply refer to the word
'God'. That word in the Bible can be used of the true God,
false gods or other nations' gods. That isn't the name being
spoken about. To understand this name, we will need to wind
further back in the book of Exodus.

Here God called Moses to be the leader through whom he
would rescue his people. In that moment of appointment,
Moses asked God a question:

> Moses said to God, 'Suppose I go to the Israelites and say
> to them, "The God of your fathers has sent me to you,"
> and they ask me, "What is his name?" Then what shall I
> tell them?'
> (Exodus 3:13)

This seems a curious request. Presumably, the Israelites know
God's name – he is after all 'the God of your fathers'.

This is where we start to see the significance of the idea of God's name. When Moses is asked, 'What is his name?', this is basically asking, 'What new revelation of God do you have?' God's name is tied up with what he does. Moses will be announcing a new venture on behalf of God, and so they'll ask what God has revealed to him.

And here's the reply:

> God said to Moses, 'I AM WHO I AM. This is what you are to say to the Israelites: "I AM has sent me to you."'
>
> God also said to Moses, 'Say to the Israelites, "The LORD, the God of your fathers – the God of Abraham, the God of Isaac and the God of Jacob – has sent me to you."
>
> 'This is my name for ever,
> > the name you shall call me
> > from generation to generation.'
> (Exodus 3:14–15)

God reveals his name as, 'I AM WHO I AM', which he shortens to 'I AM'. Then God uses the name 'The LORD' in small capitals. This is not simply a bigger version of 'Lord'! It is shorthand for the 'I AM WHO I AM' phrase. It is probably pronounced 'Yahweh'. English Bibles have used the small capitals version, 'LORD', to distinguish it from 'Lord'. The key point is that it is this name, 'The LORD', which they are to use for God. This is the name to call him from generation to generation.

So what is the significance of the name? The phrase 'I AM WHO I AM' speaks about God's self-existence and independence. But later in Exodus God explains its significance more clearly. In chapter 6, he is speaking to Moses again and explaining his rescue to come. This is how he puts it:

> God also said to Moses, 'I am the LORD. I appeared to Abraham,
> to Isaac and to Jacob as God Almighty, but by my name the LORD
> I did not make myself known to them. I also established my
> covenant with them to give them the land of Canaan, where
> they resided as foreigners. Moreover, I have heard the groaning
> of the Israelites, whom the Egyptians are enslaving, and I have
> remembered my covenant.'
> (Exodus 6:2–5)

God had made promises of rescue and the gift of the Promised
Land to Abraham, Isaac and Jacob, but they didn't see those
promises fulfilled. In that sense they didn't know God as 'the
LORD'. But now Moses and the Israelites will see God to be
the LORD:

> Therefore, say to the Israelites: 'I am the LORD, and I will bring
> you out from under the yoke of the Egyptians. I will free you
> from being slaves to them, and I will redeem you with an
> outstretched arm and with mighty acts of judgment. I will take
> you as my own people, and I will be your God. Then you will
> know that I am the LORD your God, who brought you out from
> under the yoke of the Egyptians.'
> (Exodus 6:6–7)

God is going to act; he's going to keep his promises; he will
show himself to be the LORD. And the result is that his people
will know him as the LORD.

Imagine that some friends of yours get married. You
could say, 'We've known Harry and Alison as individuals,
but now we will know them as husband or wife.' Or if
friends have children, you could say, 'We've known Mark and
Julie as a couple, but now we will know them as father
and mother.'

The new situation shows us something new about them. That's what God means when he says the previous generations didn't know him as the Lord, but this generation will. God doesn't become something new, but his people will now see this new aspect. They will know him as the covenant-keeping, redeeming, rescuing God.

So this name 'the Lord' is very special. It points to God's *faithful and gracious salvation*. It is about his commitment to his people, shown in what he has done for them. It's not simply a way of saying 'God'. Rather, it's a way of saying 'my God who has rescued me and is committed to me'. Just like the word 'father' doesn't just name a person, it sums up what that person is to you.

So God's name becomes shorthand for his covenant relationship with his people: his commitment to them and his salvation of them. This is why we are told that his people proclaim his name, exalt his name, trust in his name, praise his name, call on his name, and more. We're told: 'Holy and awesome is his name' (Psalm 111:9).

No wonder God commands, 'You shall not misuse the name of the Lord your God.'

If God's name is shorthand for his covenant relationship with his people, then for Christian believers his name is now connected to Jesus. God's promises of salvation are fulfilled in Jesus. God's new covenant is brought about through Jesus'

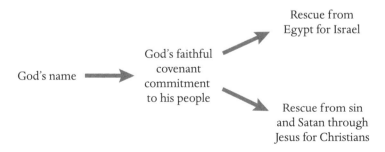

death and resurrection. When we say the 'name of the Lord', we mean the name of the 'Son of God, who loved me and gave himself for me' (Galatians 2:20).

We can picture this in the diagram on page 51.

So the 'name of God' here is not just a name; it is a way of referring to God, his commitment to you, and all he has done for you.

Honouring God rather than taking him lightly

Having looked at God's name, what does it mean to misuse it? You may know the traditional translation of that phrase is taking the Lord's name 'in vain'. It is literally 'lifting it up to vanity'. The word 'vanity' has the idea of being worthless or empty. Lifting it up is about using it, in the first instance, using it by speaking it, but as we'll see, it can be broader than that.

So people are being told, 'Do not use God's name as a worthless or empty thing.' Why not? That would be to regard God and his faithful salvation as worthless or empty. Instead, God's name should be a name they respect and honour. It should be a precious name to them, because it represents all that God is and all that he has done for them. They are being warned: don't you dare misuse that name because that would show you don't really appreciate what it stands for.

So this command is about our attitude to God and what he has done for us. His name, or the name of Jesus, should bring reverence, thankfulness and praise. It should be a name we honour, a name of substance and weightiness, which is the opposite of emptiness.

Imagine that there is a hostage situation and the SAS are called in. They mount a rescue operation with all the attendant dangers and risks. They go in and they get the hostages out; they are delivered home safe and sound.

How would those hostages now speak about the SAS? They wouldn't hear a bad word about them. They'd certainly never speak a bad word about them. They wouldn't take what they'd done lightly and so speak poorly of the name of the SAS. Instead, they'd hold them in high regard and speak well of them.

That's the idea here. We want to hold God's name in high esteem because he himself, and what he has done, is so precious to us. And as we have seen, Christians know that salvation has been achieved through the death of Jesus. We would never want to speak badly of his name.

So this commandment is a warning to us not to take God and his salvation lightly. Or, more positively, to honour God and his salvation rightly. We want there to be right respect and appreciation for who he is and what he's done. We want to treat his name with the value it deserves. Jesus taught us to pray, 'hallowed be your name' (Matthew 6:9). That is praying that God's name will be respected, that God's actions in Jesus will be rightly seen and appreciated. When we pray the Lord's Prayer, we are praying that the third commandment will be kept.

Speaking God's name

You will probably know that this command has often been understood as saying, 'Do not use God's name as a swearword', so breaking it is saying, 'Oh my God', or 'Jesus!' Well, it certainly has implications for swearing, because if we were to speak like that, it would be showing disregard for God's name rather than honouring it rightly. But it goes much further.

Let's look at some examples in the detailed laws of what this command means in practice. The worst case is where God's name is deliberately insulted and degraded: 'Anyone who uses the name of the LORD blasphemously is to be put to death' (Leviticus 24:16).

Blaspheming God's name is to deliberately speak badly of him, to bad-mouth him. It shows utter disregard for him and for what he has done. That is why the penalty is so severe in this verse, because this is a rejection of God and his salvation.

I think we see a similar attitude in Jesus' warning about blaspheming against the Holy Spirit (Mark 3:28–29). He says that is when people are seeing something done by the Holy Spirit, but deliberately attributing it to the devil. It is seeing God's salvation, and saying it is an evil thing. Such an attitude shows a deep and profound rejection of God and what he has done.

A different example is where God's name is used carelessly, so showing a disregard for how important he is. This is seen in using his name in oaths: 'Do not swear falsely by my name and so profane the name of your God. I am the LORD' (Leviticus 19:12).

This is using God's name to add to your promise. You want to make it especially clear that you mean what you say, so you add, 'I swear by the Lord.' But if you don't intend to keep the promise, you are swearing 'falsely' – that shows lack of respect for the name you've just invoked.

Today someone might say, 'I swear on my mother's grave' to add gravity to a promise. But if the person doesn't intend to keep the promise, that shows the individual has very little respect for his or her mother. So too with God. You invoke his name only when you are taking him seriously.

More positively, we're told to use God's name with serious-ness: 'Fear the LORD your God, serve him only and take your oaths in his name' (Deuteronomy 6:13). Swearing by God when you mean it is appropriate because he means so much to you – his name has appropriate weight.

So this command has implications for the way we use God's name. We speak of him as the one who is deeply meaningful to us, whose salvation is wonderfully precious to us, and so whose name is deeply significant to us. That will flow out in our conversation about God. People will pick up on how important he is to us.

This doesn't mean we have to pause and use a special voice every time we refer to God, but it will mean we are not careless or carefree in referring to him. Jesus taught us that we can call God 'Father' and so approach him with utter confidence (Matthew 6:9). But there must still be weight and honour because this is the God who is so precious to us.

I have a friend for whom this is especially true. Whenever you hear him speak about God, there is a quiet reverence and a loving passion. You can tell he is speaking about someone really significant to him. That's the right way to honour God and his name.

For Christians, of course, that is also the way to speak Jesus' name. His name sums up all that God has done for us; it is in his name that we are saved. So our use of his name should show right appreciation for what he has done. I should refer to him with reverence, love and gladness.

Gathering in God's name

Consider how obeying this commandment might affect how we gather as God's people on Sundays or at other times. We gather in his name; we sing praise to his name; we call on his name in prayer; his Word is spoken in his name to us. Think how a high view of his name will affect all that happens.

I think it means that there will be gravity to all we do. If God's name is important to us, then these activities will be important to us too. That might be shown in such simple things as being there on time – because this is important to us. It might be shown by concentration and thoughtfulness – because this is important to us. It might be shown by turning off mobile phones – because this is important to us. It will be shown by a heartfelt desire to honour God, to lift him high, to bow before him, to trust him and praise him – because he is important to us.

That doesn't mean our church meetings need be sombre, formal or boring – in fact, I am all for church that is informal and engaging! But we dare not be casual in what we are doing and take God lightly. As we sing and pray, we want a right reverence and honouring of him in our hearts.

Speaking in God's name

There is also a more specific application to God's Word being spoken – both for those who hear it and those who speak it. To the hearers first, God says, 'I myself will call to account anyone who does not listen to my words that the prophet speaks in my name' (Deuteronomy 18:19).

This says that your response to God's Word shows your response to God himself. It is his Word, spoken in his name. If we disregard it, then we are showing that we disregard him. Conversely, taking God seriously means taking his Word seriously too.

So we honour God's name in our attitude to his Word. We will want to be attentive, focused and, above all, obedient to all he says to us.

There is also a severe warning for those who speak in God's name: 'But a prophet who presumes to speak in my name anything I have not commanded, or a prophet who speaks in the name of other gods, is to be put to death' (Deuteronomy 18:20). When someone writes a letter pretending to be from someone else, we call it forgery. This is the equivalent with God: speaking something in his name when he has not said it.

Speaking in God's name is a great responsibility. You are attaching God's authority and person to what you are saying – so you'd better not say something he hasn't said. In the Old Testament, this was seen in the prophets speaking only what God had revealed to them. But it was also seen in people teaching only what was written in God's Word. And that is how it continues today: teachers and preachers must say only what God himself has said.

That means not adding to, or taking away from, God's Word. But unfortunately, false teaching exists today, just as it has done in every age. We're told to expect it (2 Peter 2:1). But every teacher who takes God's name seriously will do all he or she can to understand God's Word rightly and teach it accurately.

Living out God's name

The last way in which we honour God's name rightly is in the way we live. God says to his people:

> Keep my commands and follow them. I am the Lord. Do not profane my holy name, for I must be acknowledged as holy by the Israelites. I am the Lord, who made you holy and who brought you out of Egypt to be your God. I am the Lord.
> (Leviticus 22:31–33)

Here God's name can be 'profaned' by disobedience. God is the one who has 'made us holy' and has rescued us from slavery, and we must now acknowledge him as holy. That is shown in keeping his commands and following them.

We see the same thing later in Deuteronomy:

> If you do not carefully follow all the words of this law, which are written in this book, and do not revere this glorious and awesome name – the LORD your God . . .
> (Deuteronomy 28:58)

See how the idea of following God's laws and revering his name go together. This is like schoolchildren being told that their behaviour will reflect on the school – usually in terms of bad behaviour bringing the school down. Such bad behaviour has that effect because the children in question are wearing their school uniform – bearing the name of the school.

So too for God's people. They are known to be his people, to bear his name, and so how they live reflects on him. That's why obeying him and revering his name go together.

If his name is important to us, if we take him and what he has done for us seriously, then we will take his commands seriously too. But if we have a 'take it or leave it' attitude to God's commands, then we will have a 'take him or leave him' attitude to God himself and his salvation in Jesus.

Responding to God

This commandment can be broken by our speech and our actions. It involves how we use God's name and what is attached to his name. But fundamentally, it is about our attitude to God and the salvation he offers: do we take that seriously? Is it important to us? If it is, then we will hate the thought of misusing his name.

If we are convicted by this command, then once again the first thing we must do is remember that Jesus obeyed this command for us. He always honoured God's name; he never took his name lightly. He obeyed on our behalf, and then he died in our place.

So first, we run to Jesus. And second, we ask for God's help to live as we should, requesting help in seeing how wonderfully precious his name is – because he is so precious and his salvation in Jesus is so precious. And as we see all that, we will want to honour and treasure his name in our words and actions. We will surely pray, 'Hallowed be your name.'

4. CELEBRATING SALVATION

In the film *Chariots of Fire*, the runner Eric Liddell refuses to run in the heats for his 100-m race because it is held on a Sunday. He is heavily pressured by the British Olympic Committee to take part, but he stands firm. His refusal to run because of his Christian convictions made headlines around the world.

Earlier in the film Eric had seen a lad kicking a football around on a Sunday and gently tells him off: 'The Sabbath's not a day for playing football, is it?' 'No,' the boy reluctantly agrees.

Liddell's Christian commitment is wonderful to see, especially in the face of pressure and criticism. But was he right?

Christians have long debated the meaning of the fourth commandment for today. Is it 'You shall not work on Saturdays', or is it 'You shall not play on Sundays'? Or is it something else?

Here's the original command:

Remember the Sabbath day by keeping it holy. Six days you shall labour and do all your work, but the seventh day is a sabbath to the LORD your God. On it you shall not do any work, neither you, nor your son or daughter, nor your male or female servant, nor your animals, nor any foreigner residing in your towns.
(Exodus 20:8–10)

A day that is different

The command is to do with the 'Sabbath day', that is, the seventh day of the week, which is Saturday. This day is to be 'remembered' by keeping it 'holy', which means it was set apart as different. And the way it was kept holy was by not working on it. The chain of thought is outlined in the diagram here.

Remember the Sabbath day → Keep it holy (separate or special) → So don't do any work

The command is very clear on not working: neither you, nor any family member, nor any servant is to do any work. You can't even get a foreigner who doesn't believe in God to do some cooking for you on the Sabbath. You can't even leave your ox wandering round the field dragging a plough. This was a day of total shutdown.

The idea of stopping is actually there in the word 'Sabbath' itself: it comes from a word that means stop or cease. So the Sabbath is the 'stopping day'.

This doesn't actually mean no work at all would be done. A moment's thought tells us that some 'work' must be done on the Sabbath: cows still need milking; people and animals need feeding. In fact, as the Old Testament goes on, we see some specific exceptions: the priests still worked in the sanctuary (e.g. Leviticus 24:1–3; Numbers 28:9–10), and the army still had detachments of soldiers on guard (2 Kings 11:5–7). So the command is to cease from work as far as possible; they were not to do anything that could have been done on the other six days.

We see one example of this in commands for the Passover festival. On the first and last days of the feast, which were 'Sabbaths', the people are told: 'Do no work at all on these days, except to prepare food for everyone to eat; that is all you may do' (Exodus 12:16).

In practice, this command meant not collecting wood (Numbers 15:32), not lighting fires (Exodus 35:3, possibly referring to starting new fires rather than keeping one going), not buying or selling goods (Nehemiah 10:31), not treading a winepress or transporting goods (Nehemiah 13:15; Jeremiah 17:21). These were unnecessary and could be done on other days. So to do them on the Sabbath was to show disregard for God's command by treating this day like any other.

This command was to be observed even during the ploughing and harvesting season when the pressure to work would be high (Exodus 34:21). So this was a special day, marked out from the rest of the week. People were to think about it differently and live differently too.

We should notice that, as with other commands, this wasn't supposed to be purely a matter of external obedience. God speaks about people's attitude to his Sabbath as well:

> 'If you keep your feet from breaking the Sabbath
>   and from doing as you please on my holy day,
> if you call the Sabbath a delight
>   and the LORD's holy day honourable,
> and if you honour it by not going your own way
>   and not doing as you please or speaking idle words,

then you will find your joy in the Lord,
   and I will cause you to ride in triumph on the heights
      of the land
   and to feast on the inheritance of your father Jacob.'
               For the mouth of the Lord has spoken.
(Isaiah 58:13–14)

The Sabbath was not supposed to be a harsh restriction; it was to be a delight! Your attitude to the Sabbath showed your attitude to God – it is *his* Sabbath. You honoured the day because you wanted to honour him. And the result was blessing from God.

Elsewhere God has a go at people who observe the Sabbath but long for it to be over so they can start trading again (Amos 8:5). That's 'obeying' the command, but seeing it as a hindrance and restriction rather than a delight.

Sabbath as a sign

The Sabbath really was a big deal for Israel. God commands its observance in the strictest terms, and its abuse is one of the commonly mentioned reasons for his punishment of his people. So the Sabbath is much more than a day off.

This becomes clearer later in Exodus where the Sabbath is spoken of as a sign of the covenant:

Then the Lord said to Moses, 'Say to the Israelites, "You must observe my Sabbaths. This will be a *sign between me and you* for the generations to come, so that you may know that I am the Lord, who makes you holy.

'"Observe the Sabbath, because it is holy to you. Anyone who desecrates it is to be put to death; those who do any work on that

day must be cut off from their people. For six days work is to
be done, but the seventh day is a day of sabbath rest, holy to the
LORD. Whoever does any work on the Sabbath day is to be put
to death. The Israelites are to observe the Sabbath, celebrating it
for the generations to come as a lasting covenant. It will be a *sign
between me and the Israelites* for ever, for in six days the LORD made
the heavens and the earth, and on the seventh day he rested and
was refreshed."'

(Exodus 31:12–17, italics mine)

Note the repetition that the Sabbath is a sign between God
and his people. It's as if they have a special meaningful sign
between them, and it's the Sabbath day.

It is specifically a sign so that they will know he is the LORD
who makes them holy. This is repeated elsewhere: 'Also I gave
them my Sabbaths as a sign between us, so they would know
that I the Lord made them holy' (Ezekiel 20:12).

Being made holy is about being placed in a special relationship with God, being set apart specifically for him. So this is
speaking about the special covenant relationship Israel had,
that they were God's people and he was their God. As they
stopped working for that day, it should have reminded them
that they were God's special people; he'd chosen them and
made them his own.

That's why the penalties for breaking the Sabbath are so
severe – being put to death. Breaking the Sabbath was saying
you didn't want to be part of God's holy people, that you
didn't want a covenant relationship with him.

Why have a rest?

Back in Exodus 20 the reason for the Sabbath is given like
this:

For in six days the LORD made the heavens and the earth, the sea, and all that is in them, but he rested on the seventh day. Therefore the LORD blessed the Sabbath day and made it holy.
(Exodus 20:11)

This looks back to the story of creation, where we are told that God rested on the seventh day, and so he blessed that day and made it holy. So the Sabbath is part of the pattern of creation. We are not made as machines that keep working 24/7; we need rest and recuperation. In Exodus 31 (quoted above), it even says that God himself 'rested and was refreshed'. That is what we need too: rest and refreshment.

We see this in some of the reasons that are given for Sabbath rest:

Six days do your work, but on the seventh day do not work, so that your ox and your donkey may rest, and so that the slave born in your household and the foreigner living among you may be refreshed.
(Exodus 23:12)

We need time off to rest and be 'refreshed' – literally to draw breath. This is simply part of how God has made us, and we must live within the limits of our humanity.

However, when the Ten Commandments are repeated in Deuteronomy, a different reason is given:

Observe the Sabbath day by keeping it holy, as the LORD your God has commanded you. Six days you shall labour and do all your work . . . Remember that you were slaves in Egypt and that the LORD your God brought you out of there with a mighty hand and an outstretched arm. Therefore the LORD your God has commanded you to observe the Sabbath day.
(Deuteronomy 5:12–15)

There is a connection here that we don't readily pick up in English: when it says 'six days you shall labour', it uses the same word as for being a 'slave' in Egypt. So it is like saying, 'Six days you shall slave . . . remember you were slaves'. The Sabbath rest is a reminder of release from slavery.

Here Sabbath is connected to salvation: they are to rest from their work to remember that God rescued them.

This connection is reinforced through the use of 'rest' elsewhere in the Old Testament. The Promised Land in particular is spoken of as the people's 'resting place' and where God will give them 'rest' (Deuteronomy 12:9–10). So 'rest' is more than a sit-down; it is a picture of the harmony of salvation that God will give his people.

This use of 'rest' to picture the harmony of salvation is also seen in some other laws too. God said the land itself should have a Sabbath rest where crops weren't grown every seven years. Then, every seventh of these Sabbath years (every forty-nine years), there was to be a mega-Sabbath, called the Year of Jubilee (see Leviticus 25). Not only was the land to be given rest, but there was a 'resetting' of everyone's inheritance in the land. Any land that had been sold was restored to the family of its original owners. Anyone who had become a slave because of poverty was released.

God finishes these instructions by saying, 'They are my servants, whom I brought out of Egypt. I am the LORD your God' (Leviticus 25:55).

So this 'mega-Sabbath' was like going back to the moment when they had just entered the land and everyone owned their own land and everyone was free. It was recapturing the moment of God's salvation and gift of rest.

The diagram opposite helps draw this together. The command for the Sabbath comes from both the pattern of creation and the work of salvation. The 'rest' that is being

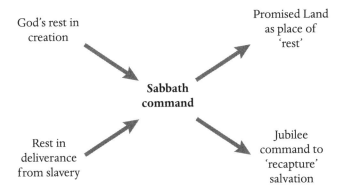

given is a picture of the harmony of creation, the harmony that God gave the people when they entered the Promised Land.

This shows us that 'Sabbath' and 'rest' do not simply mean having a break from work (although they include that); they picture the wonderful rest God gives his people through his salvation.

This is why the command tells Israel to 'remember' the Sabbath. By having a special day when they stopped working, they were remembering what God had done for them and the rest he offered them. They were celebrating their salvation.

The sign fulfilled

This meaning of Sabbath and rest is then confirmed in the New Testament. First, we have Jesus' wonderful words:

> Come to me, all you who are weary and burdened, and I will give you rest. Take my yoke upon you and learn from me, for I am gentle and humble in heart, and you will find rest for your souls. For my yoke is easy and my burden is light.
> (Matthew 11:28–30)

Jesus is not saying he'll give us a break in a busy and stressful life. He is claiming to come as the true source of rest. He is the provider of the true Sabbath. The sign was only ever pointing to him. So we 'come to him' to receive rest for our souls.

The apostle Paul speaks about Old Testament laws, including Sabbaths, as shadows that are fulfilled in Jesus:

> Therefore do not let anyone judge you by what you eat or drink, or with regard to a religious festival, a New Moon celebration or a Sabbath day. These are a shadow of the things that were to come; the reality, however, is found in Christ.
> (Colossians 2:16–17)

The Sabbath is a shadow of what was to come. Shadows have the same shape and outline as the real thing, but they are only shadows in the end. So the Sabbath pictured rest, but it wasn't the real thing. The reality comes in the true rest that Jesus brings.

Lastly, the book of Hebrews speaks about the entry into the Promised Land as 'entering rest'. The author goes on to speak about how we can enter that rest by believing the gospel:

> There remains, then, a Sabbath-rest for the people of God; for anyone who enters God's rest also rests from their works, just as God did from his. Let us, therefore, make every effort to enter that rest, so that no one will perish by following their example of disobedience.
> (Hebrews 4:9–11)

This means that we enter the Sabbath rest God offers by trusting in Jesus.

The Sabbath command then has more to do with celebrating salvation than stopping working. But in the Old Testament celebrating salvation was shown precisely by stopping working. By ceasing from their toil, the people remembered that God had saved them from slavery, that they were made for more than work, that he offered them true rest.

What should we do on Sundays?

So where does that leave us today?

We've seen that there is a 'creation' reason for the Sabbath – that we need rest and refreshment. And we've seen there is a 'salvation' reason for the Sabbath – it celebrated God's rescue and his provision of rest. That salvation reason was a sign that is fulfilled in Jesus, so we now enter God's rest by believing the gospel.

Most people would agree with that, but there have still been huge variations and disagreements on what we should do in practice. Should we regard Saturday or Sunday as special? Is Sunday a new 'Christian Sabbath'? Should we work, shop or play on Sundays? Whole books are written on this, so I'm not going to be able to fit all the arguments in here. Instead, I'll make some observations and suggestions.

First, I think that the Sabbath command is the one that is most changed from the Old Testament. It was a specific sign of the old covenant, which is why it was enforced so strongly then. Its fulfilment in Christ means it does not operate the same way today.

However, we should still rest. The need for recuperation and refreshment remains. The creation pattern of one day off in seven, while no longer being law as it was for Israel, remains wisdom today. In other words, the fulfilment of the sign doesn't mean that there's an end to the practice. Jesus is indeed our true 'rest', but we still need to take a break. So the 'creation' reason for the Sabbath remains.

Second, we should still celebrate our salvation. The Sabbath day was a day away from the toil of work, affected as it is by the fall, and so a day to remember and celebrate God's redemption from slavery. The Sabbath pointed to the promise of 'rest' from God, and we now have that rest in Christ and look forward to its fulfilment in the new creation. And a day of rest from work is still a way of celebrating that salvation. In fact, we could say that we have reason for even more celebration and anticipation of our final rest. We should regard time off very seriously indeed.

Some would also say that a time off on Sundays is a chance to meet with God and his people. There are two issues wrapped together here. First, there's the question of whether the Sabbath and gathering as God's people were put together. Was it a day for rest, or a day for rest and worship? I think the focus is a day of rest. The command in the Old Testament is focused on not working; it doesn't command religious gatherings (and the only reference to one is in Leviticus 23:2). Certainly, Christians in the first centuries of the church had to work on Sundays, which didn't become a day off until the fourth century.

The second issue is whether Christians should gather on Sundays. They certainly should gather regularly, but does it need to be a Sunday? Some suggest that Christians started meeting on Sundays in the evenings after work. The thinking is that Sunday was the day to meet in order to celebrate Jesus' resurrection.

However, there is virtually nothing that describes this in the New Testament, let alone commands it. The main example is in Acts 20:7 where Paul meets with the Christians in Troas on a Sunday evening to break bread. But we don't know if that was because it was the day when he happened to be there (he was passing through) or because it was their regular day of meeting. There is reference in Revelation 1:10 to the 'Lord's Day', but we're not told which day that was. It is often understood to be a reference to Sundays, but even if that's so, there's no reference to what Christians should or should not do on that day.

What is certainly true is that as Christian communities spread, meeting on Sundays became standard. But that happened even when Sunday was a regular workday, and so it was separated from their rest day. If our society makes Sunday a standard day off, then that is also a great day to meet together as God's people. So I'm very happy with Sunday church! But I don't think it is required.

We've covered a number of connected issues: should we take a day off from work every week (a Sabbath), and if so, which day should it be, and should Christians specifically gather to meet on Sundays?

We should be aware that there are lots of different positions on these issues.

- Some think that Christians should still take Saturday off, and no unnecessary work should be done. This is also the day for church gathering (Seventh-Day Adventists and Seventh Day Baptists).
- Some think that Sunday should be a day off for everyone, with no unnecessary work to be done, and for meeting as church ('Sabbatarians').
- Some think that fulfilment in Christ means there is flexibility, even if it remains wise and convenient to take Sundays as a day off work and often as a time to meet as church too.

Paul's comment in Romans 14 should warn us about being too condemning of other people's positions here: 'One person considers one day more sacred than another; another considers every day alike. Each of them should be fully convinced in their own mind' (Romans 14:5).

Paul's comment here comes in a section on 'disputable matters', which mainly focuses on eating certain foods. But this comment on days, while not mentioning Sabbaths, would still seem to apply to them. Some people, especially from a Jewish background, could easily have regarded one day more highly than others, while other people, probably from a Gentile background, didn't. Paul doesn't legislate, and is more concerned that people live out their own convictions.

Responding to God

So where does that leave you and me?

We should take time off. Many people work too hard, and their families, their spiritual lives and their health can suffer as a result. You need to know that God made us for more than work. The Sabbath was a gift to be enjoyed, that would result in flourishing. Some people need to embrace that more. This means being more serious about rest.

Too many of us check our work emails during our time off, whether it's evenings, weekends or holidays. In fact, we are never really 'off' work. We need to learn how to rest properly rather than have low-grade rest where we're really still in work mode. This may well mean engaging in creation and creativity with more purpose, whether it be in walks, hobbies, sports, arts, or whatever else we like. Rest is not 'killing time'; it's resting from work and enjoying other parts of life.

We should also celebrate God's salvation and the rest that Jesus provides. We celebrate that in many ways, but one key way is in resting. And that requires a change of mindset. As you sit back, or go for a stroll, or play some sport, remember that Jesus has won rest for you. He has freed you from slavery. Your regular rest now can celebrate that and anticipate the great rest to come.

And as you work too hard, and fail to celebrate salvation, remember Jesus did these things perfectly for you. He never broke the Sabbath command, despite being accused of doing so. He comes as Lord of the Sabbath. He comes to bring perfect rest and invites us to join him in it.

5. HONOURING PARENTS

How do you feel about your parents?

There will be a wide range of responses to that question. Some will be very positive: you may feel appreciation, love, warmth and respect. Unfortunately, other responses will be negative: exasperation, frustration, anger or bitterness. Different feelings will then be shown in how you speak to (or don't speak to) your parents and how you treat them.

At best, parents are honoured; at worst, they are demeaned.

And a whole variety of factors will affect how you answer the question above.

It will depend on your age and stage of life: for example, your relationship with your parents when you are twenty is very different from when you are fifty.

It will depend on the culture in which you've grown up: some cultures treat elderly parents with great respect, while others are closer to mockery. We will have learned from our culture even subconsciously. There is the culture of individual families too, with some speaking well of grandparents, while others joke about them behind their backs.

It will depend too on your particular situation: some parents live nearby and are seen regularly, while others are far away and visits are infrequent. Some are in good health, some in a care home. Some function well, while others struggle with email and insurance letters. Some are well off, while others need financial support. All these factors, and more, affect the shape of our relationship with our parents.

Lastly, but most importantly of all, it will depend on your experience of your parents. Some of us respond to our parents with warmth and appreciation, because they've been good parents and we know it only too well. Even if they drive us crazy sometimes, we still love and respect them.

Unfortunately, others have had very painful experiences: parents who have left the family, been absent, unkind, manipulating and, at worst, abusive. And our instinctive reaction can readily and understandably be anger, sadness and fear. We most easily hate them, or simply want to ignore them, rather than honour them.

We will need to be fully aware of those different factors as we look at this command. Obeying it will be a challenge for all of us, but our different experiences and backgrounds will make it a very different challenge for each one of us.

So take a moment to reflect: how do you feel towards your parents? What factors drive your reaction?

So far, the commands God has given us have been directed primarily towards him – they've been examples of how we love him as our God and Saviour. Now the commands turn to how we think about, and live with, one another, and the first one is about parents: 'Honour your father and your mother, so that you may live long in the land the LORD your God is giving you' (Exodus 20:12).

Look up to your parents

This is a command to look up to your parents, to give them a right respect and esteem. The word 'honour' is used when there is a difference between people's status or seniority, for example in the case of a leader being honoured by his followers, a master by his servants, and even God by his people. So this command means acknowledging that your parents are not on the same level as you; they deserve recognition and respect simply because they are your parents.

Notice that God makes sure to include both father and mother in this command. In the Bible, the father is often given particular responsibility as the head of the household, but both father and mother are to be honoured equally.

Notice too that there are no age limits put on this command. It is not only to small children, not only while you live at home with your parents, and not only when they are old and need help. It applies to all of us throughout life. Even when our parents have died, our attitude to them still remains in the way we think about them and speak of them.

Warning against disrespect

We see some of what this honouring looks like, or rather doesn't look like, in later laws and parts of the Old Testament. The worst case is when someone utterly rejects their parents by attacking them or cursing them: 'Anyone who attacks their father or mother is to be put to death . . . Anyone who curses their father or mother is to be put to death' (Exodus 21:15, 17).

It can also be shown in stubborn rebellion against parents:

> If someone has a stubborn and rebellious son who does not
> obey his father and mother and will not listen to them when

they discipline him, his father and mother shall take hold
of him and bring him to the elders at the gate of his town.
They shall say to the elders, 'This son of ours is stubborn
and rebellious. He will not obey us. He is a glutton and a
drunkard.'
(Deuteronomy 21:18–20)

This son should have looked up to his parents by listening to
them and obeying them, but he did the opposite. Persistent,
wilful disrespect of parents was taken very seriously indeed.

Similarly, in Proverbs, acting against your parents is warned
against:

> Whoever robs their father and drives out their mother
>   is a child who brings shame and disgrace.
> (Proverbs 19:26)

Similarly, mocking or scorning will be punished:

> The eye that mocks a father,
>   that scorns an aged mother,
> will be pecked out by the ravens of the valley,
>   will be eaten by the vultures.
> (Proverbs 30:17)

I'm not sure why the punishment is having your eye pecked
out and eaten by birds, but the point is clear: we are not to do
anything that looks down on or belittles our parents.

By comparison, we need to recognize that mocking parents
is pretty standard in Western culture. It is accepted as part
of humour, advertising and social convention. We laugh at
embarrassing dad stories. We express exasperation at mums
who can't work their new phones.

The call to honour

As well as the warning against disrespect, there are positive calls to respect parents: 'Each of you must respect your mother and father' (Leviticus 19:3).

This respect is shown in how they are to be listened to. So in Proverbs we read:

> My son, keep your father's command
> and do not forsake your mother's teaching.
> (Proverbs 6:20)

> Listen to your father, who gave you life,
> and do not despise your mother when she is old.
> (Proverbs 23:22)

This attitude of respect is shown here particularly in listening to what they say. You regard your parents' advice as worth hearing and following. This means acknowledging that they know more about life than you do. Compare that to the standard teenage reaction of thinking that your parents are hopelessly out of touch. These words, often attributed to Mark Twain, express this well:

> When I was a boy of fourteen, my father was so ignorant I could hardly stand to have the old man around. But when I got to be twenty-one, I was astonished at how much the old man had learned in seven years.

Many of us would say that that process doesn't stop in our early twenties either. As we get older, we can often see the wisdom that our parents always had. This is a command to believe that and so listen to our parents throughout life.

All through the book of Proverbs there is a picture of respecting, listening to and following your parents:

> A wise son heeds his father's instruction,
>   but a mocker does not respond to rebukes.
> (Proverbs 13:1)

> A wise son brings joy to his father,
>   but a foolish man despises his mother.
> (Proverbs 15:20)

Our attitude is to be one of lifting our parents up rather than putting them down, listening to them rather than rejecting them, and honouring them rather than despising them.

Why honour parents?

Why is this so important? Why include it in the Ten Commandments?

Two reasons, I think. First is the importance of the family. God has made us to live in families where parents have the role of teaching, guiding and disciplining. God has designed families to work where parents lead and children follow. In fact, the call to honour and respect parents is echoed in the call to honour and respect God himself. So it is as if the parents are God's representatives in the family. As they teach, guide and discipline, they act as a channel for God's authority.

By comparison, it is not uncommon today to hear that parents do not have such authority over their children. Parents and children are simply equal members of the family, we're told, and so parents are not to be looked up to in this way. How do we respond to such thinking? We must affirm that God has made everyone equal in dignity and value – a parent is no more important than a child in that respect. But we must also affirm that God's design is that real leadership is exercised by parents. And so they are to be honoured in this way. We should never be embarrassed about God's pattern for the family.

The second reason why this was so important within Israel was because of the connection with people's relationship with God. The parents were to teach their children about God: his promises, his rescue and his covenant relationship with them. Here's how it's expressed in a later psalm:

> My people, hear my teaching;
>> listen to the words of my mouth.
> I will open my mouth with a parable;
>> I will utter hidden things, things from of old –
> things we have heard and known,
>> things our ancestors have told us.
> We will not hide them from their descendants;
>> we will tell the next generation
> the praiseworthy deeds of the LORD,
>> his power, and the wonders he has done.
> He decreed statutes for Jacob
>> and established the law in Israel,
> which he commanded our ancestors
>> to teach their children,
> so that the next generation would know them,
>> even the children yet to be born,
>> and they in turn would tell their children.
> Then they would put their trust in God
>> and would not forget his deeds
>> but would keep his commands.
> They would not be like their ancestors –
>> a stubborn and rebellious generation,

whose hearts were not loyal to God,
  whose spirits were not faithful to him.
(Psalm 78:1–8)

We saw above that rejection of parents was punished severely. One reason was that it was taken to be a sign of rejecting God and his salvation. That's why there is a promise attached to the command: 'Honour your father and your mother, so that you may live long in the land the LORD your God is giving you' (Exodus 20:12).

Long life in the land would come to them if they kept the covenant with God. But that would only happen if they honoured their parents and the covenant teaching was passed on from one generation to another.

Life as children

In applying this to ourselves, we'll think mainly about our life as children. In Ephesians, we read: 'Children, obey your parents in the Lord, for this is right. "Honour your father and mother"' (Ephesians 6:1–2).

The command isn't quoted, but the same sentiment is given in Colossians: 'Children, obey your parents in everything, for this pleases the Lord' (Colossians 3:20).

So this command still applies to Christians today. There is still an expectation of children honouring their parents. When children are young, that basically means obeying their parents. Hence, Paul says, 'obey your parents': you assume they know better and so you follow their instruction.

Jesus himself sets us an example in his submissiveness to his parents: 'Then he went down to Nazareth with them and was obedient to them' (Luke 2:51).

This simple obedience starts to change as children grow

older. So through the teenage years obedience should still be there, but there will be a growing freedom and responsibility. There will still be simple instructions ('You need to help unload the dishwasher'; 'You are coming to church'), but you will often start to have more of a discussion ('What time will you get in from the party?' 'Should you get that Saturday job?'). But even then, once the decision is made, you will stick to what your parents have said.

Increasingly, this honour will show itself in the way we talk about our parents. Teenagers and even students need to be careful, because it is very common to talk your parents down: 'They don't understand'; 'They're so rubbish'. We should beware of such comments that express contempt for our parents.

Then we will eventually leave home and become independent. We may have families of our own, but we don't stop honouring our parents. We will now make decisions for ourselves in buying a car or a house, or obtaining a job, but we should still ask for, and listen to, their opinions and advice. We may now teach our parents about the latest gadget or do practical tasks for them, but we will do so in a respectful way.

Again, the way we talk about our parents is key because it shows our attitude. It doesn't mean that we can't recognize our parents' failings, or that we can't laugh together about their foibles. And I certainly don't mean that we can't be honest and open about the pains and hurts there might be. But we still try to look up to them, rather than down on them. We will avoid the temptation to mock or despise them.

As parents become elderly, this honouring will often show itself in practical care. Jesus applies the fifth command in exactly this way. He is talking to a group of religious leaders and taking them to task for ducking out of obeying this command:

Jesus replied, '. . . God said, "Honour your father and mother"
and "Anyone who curses their father or mother is to be put to
death." But you say that if anyone declares that what might have
been used to help their father or mother is "devoted to God,"
they are not to "honour their father or mother" with it. Thus
you nullify the word of God for the sake of your tradition.'
(Matthew 15:3–6)

This was at a time where there weren't pension schemes or
social security. In your old age, you looked to your children
to provide for you. But the religious leaders had come up with
a 'get-out clause'. They could say that money was 'devoted to
God', and so they couldn't then use it to care for their parents.
So even if the care-home bills were mounting up, children
would say, 'Sorry, Mum, but all the money I have is promised
to God so I can't use it to help you out.' So Jesus says here that
they are ducking God's command or 'nullifying' it.

This means that Jesus sees the care of parents in their old
age as a prime example of honouring them. In fact, Jesus
himself, when dying on the cross, asks John, one of his disciples,
to care for his mother (John 19:26–27). He is honouring her.

What this care will look like will vary hugely, depending
on the situation. It surely should mean that we should consider
elderly or ill parents living with us. Elsewhere in the world
that is accepted as normal, while our Western culture often
shudders at the thought.

This doesn't mean that retirement or nursing homes are a
bad idea; in many cases they might be a good or a needed
option. But let's not assume that. Moreover, once in such a
home, let's show our parents honour in our level of interest,
involvement and visits. This is particularly important for us
in a culture that easily regards elderly parents as a burden to
be dealt with rather than people to be honoured.

We must remember of course that there are limits to what honouring our parents will mean in practice. It does not mean that we will always agree with them or will always obey them. Once an adult, Jesus didn't always obey his parents, but he did always honour them.

So honour your parents. Look up to them. Talk to them. Affirm them. Appreciate them.

Difficult times in which to honour parents

There are at least two particular situations in which it is very hard to honour parents.

The first is when they put pressure on us not to live for Jesus, usually because they are not converted themselves, or even if they are, they are not encouraging full-blooded discipleship.

We must remember that our allegiance to Jesus comes above allegiance to parents. Jesus said, 'Anyone who loves their father or mother more than me is not worthy of me; anyone who loves their son or daughter more than me is not worthy of me' (Matthew 10:37).

We have a higher loyalty than to our parents – to Jesus – and so we always love and obey him above them. This will mean disobeying our parents if obedience to them would mean disobedience to Jesus. It is not always that clear-cut, but that is the principle.

This is especially an issue for cultures other than Western ones. Cultural esteem of parents can be so strong that it causes real problems when someone is converted. In many Eastern cultures, family loyalty is highly prized, and huge pressure can be put on a child either not to convert to Christianity or, having done so, not to live that out in a meaningful way. In such situations, parents must still be honoured, but they must not be obeyed.

The other situation in which honouring parents is really hard is when you do not feel they deserve such honour. This can happen for a variety of reasons, but the worst cases are where they have treated you badly. The instinctive reaction is right: they do not deserve honour. This is such a painful area with such deep hurts. Parents have let us down and at worst abused their position over us. But even within such painful situations we need to say that the command still stands.

There is a parallel here with biblical commands for other 'authority' figures. Christians are told, for example, to respect their governments, and to do so even when they are not worthy of respect (Romans 13:1–7). Christian slaves are told to respect their masters, and to do so even when they are not worthy of respect (1 Peter 2:18–19). So I believe we are called to honour parents even when they are not deserving of such honour. We do so because of their position, not because of their merit.

I do not mean that we are blind to their faults, and I certainly do not mean that we deny what they may have done and how much it has hurt us. Nor will we never raise such issues with them. And of course such background will influence how we relate to them, how often we see them, and so on. But within that relationship, difficult as it is, we will still try to honour them.

Life as parents

Let's think secondly of what this means for life as parents. This command is addressed primarily to children, but it has implications for how parents should act.

We read earlier:

My son, keep your father's command
    and do not forsake your mother's teaching.
(Proverbs 6:20)

This is a call to children to listen. But it implies that parents must be teaching and commanding.

Parents must also be exercising discipline:

> A rod and a reprimand impart wisdom,
> but a child left undisciplined disgraces its mother.
> (Proverbs 29:15)

If parents don't discipline their children, then they are partly to blame for the lack of honour and obedience that results.

This is why in Ephesians 6 when the apostle Paul tells children to obey and honour their parents, he immediately goes on to say, 'Fathers, do not exasperate your children; instead, bring them up in the training and instruction of the Lord' (Ephesians 6:4).

Children are to honour and obey, but parents, and especially fathers, are to instruct and discipline. And they are to do so in a way that helps their children honour them. Fathers are being told, 'Don't drive your children crazy by being unreasonable; don't be heavy-handed, unloving or provoking.'

So parents are to parent in a way which *enables and encourages* honouring.

Think of the army where soldiers have to obey a superior officer, whether he's a good officer or not. You respect the uniform, they say, not the man. But think how much easier it is to obey a superior whom you respect, one who doesn't make unreasonable demands, a superior who isn't a soft touch, but who cares for his men and women. Such a superior helps them obey him by playing his part. So too with parents.

Of course, I don't mean that families are like army units. I mean that while children remain responsible to honour us, we will help shape their responses by how we act.

This means we will begin by simply expecting to be honoured and responding appropriately. When a young child shows disrespect, we respond with discipline. It must be loving and gentle, but it must be there. We don't let disrespect go unchecked, because that would communicate that it's OK.

This means that when you give warnings to your children – 'Do that again and this will happen' – you will follow through. Otherwise, we're teaching our children that our threats mean nothing, and that's not helping them to honour us. But this is something our culture has lost. I regularly hear parents saying 'No', often combined with threats, but then giving in or giving up too easily.

There is a word to fathers in particular here. You need to take the lead. Expect honour yourself. And discipline when it's not there. Teach this command to your children. And teach them to respect their mother. Don't leave her to do all the heavy lifting.

And this applies to all of us in church life, even if we don't have children or they have grown up. We can all help set a culture where we expect children to honour parents. The way we speak about parents and children, and the way we interact, will either support and help, or undermine this.

I remember hearing one adult gently say to a child, 'Your mum is talking to you; you should listen to her.' That comment helped to support the mum. But I also remember a time when a child was being disobedient, and someone saying to the parent, 'Kids will be kids, won't they?' They were trying to be sympathetic, but that comment undermined the role of the parents.

Responding to God

As children, we must honour our parents. As parents, we must help our children honour us.

As with each of these commands, whenever we become aware of our failures, we remind ourselves of Jesus' success. He kept these commands perfectly, and did so for us, to die in our place and so to bring us forgiveness. As we are convicted of our failures, we celebrate Jesus' work and commit ourselves once again to living according to God's pattern for life.

If you are struggling to honour your parents, remember that Jesus knew what it was to have parents act badly and misunderstand him. His parents once thought he'd gone mad and went to take charge of him (Mark 3:21). He sympathizes with you.

If you are struggling to parent your children, remember that God knows what it is to have a disobedient child who doesn't honour him. That is what Israel was (Malachi 1:6) and what many of us are. He sympathizes with you.

These commands can be hard, but we must believe they are good. God knows best. So he sympathizes with our struggles, and he urges us on.

6. RESPECTING LIFE

Everyone agrees with the sixth commandment: 'You shall not murder.'

It seems pretty simple and straightforward – don't kill anyone. And we all agree, and very few of us feel guilty, because we've never killed anyone and don't intend to. So you might think this could be a pretty short chapter.

But it's not so simple though. Consider the issues raised:

- What does this mean for terminating pregnancies – is that murder?
- What does this mean for killing in war – is that murder?
- What does this mean for capital punishment – is that murder?
- What does this mean for accidental deaths – are they ever murder?
- What does this mean for areas of negligence resulting in death – is that ever murder?

- What does this mean for suicide – assisted or otherwise – is that murder?

Rather than a short chapter, this is one of the longest, because these are involved issues. So I need to warn you now that I will be saying something about all of them, but not enough to do all of them justice.

And we will soon see that the sixth commandment goes beyond these debated topics and lands straight in our own hearts. We might not have killed anyone, but God's commandments apply to all of us and expose our hearts and attitudes.

This is what God says: 'You shall not murder' (Exodus 20:13).

No unjust taking of life

The word used for 'murder' needs some careful thought. It can be used of the deliberate action to kill someone, which we would usually call 'murder' (e.g. 1 Kings 21:19). But it can also be used of unintentional deaths by accident (e.g. Deuteronomy 4:42). And we should note that it is not the word used of killing someone in capital punishment or in war.

So we have a translation problem. Translating it as 'murder' is a bit narrower than it really is, making it sound only like a deliberate crime. Translating it as 'kill' is broader than it really is, making it sound like no killing is ever allowed. English translations have to choose one of these two options, but neither is ideal. What is being outlawed is the unjustified taking of someone's life.

We quickly see some of the actions that are being prohibited in the more detailed Old Testament laws. So first, 'murder' in a deliberate sense is clearly included:

> Anyone who strikes a person with a fatal blow is to be put
> to death . . . if anyone schemes and kills someone deliberately,
> that person is to be taken from my altar and put to death.
> (Exodus 21:12–14)

Any deliberate taking of life is outlawed and is punished by death. The reference to being taken from the altar probably envisages the person clinging on to God's altar as a place of refuge (see 1 Kings 1:50–51). If the person who is hit and dies is someone's slave, then the individual who hit the slave is still to be punished, even though the slave is his or her property (Exodus 21:20).

The issue of motive is seen to be important:

> If anyone with malice aforethought pushes another or throws
> something at them intentionally so that they die or if out
> of enmity one person hits another with their fist so that the
> other dies, that person is to be put to death; that person is
> a murderer.
> (Numbers 35:20–21)

But this is different from unintentional actions:

> But if without enmity someone suddenly pushes another or
> throws something at them unintentionally or, without seeing
> them, drops on them a stone heavy enough to kill them, and
> they die, then since that other person was not an enemy and
> no harm was intended, the assembly must judge between the
> accused and the avenger of blood according to these regulations.
> (Numbers 35:22–24)

It is not that the person bears no guilt here, but a judgment must be made as to what responsibility he or she bears.

God specifically designated certain cities as 'cities of refuge'. When an accidental death took place, the person involved could flee to one of these and be protected:

> This is the rule concerning anyone who kills a person and flees there for safety – anyone who kills a neighbour unintentionally, without malice aforethought. For instance, a man may go into the forest with his neighbour to cut wood, and as he swings his axe to fell a tree, the head may fly off and hit his neighbour and kill him. That man may flee to one of these cities and save his life.
> (Deuteronomy 19:4–5)

The flying axe head was just one example of a truly accidental death that the courts would have to expand on. But these cities couldn't be used by true murderers:

> But if out of hate someone lies in wait, assaults and kills a neighbour, and then flees to one of these cities, the killer shall be sent for by the town elders, be brought back from the city, and be handed over to the avenger of blood to die.
> (Deuteronomy 19:11–12)

However, those causing unintended death or injury are not necessarily free from responsibility. For example:

> If people are fighting and hit a pregnant woman and she gives birth prematurely but there is no serious injury, the offender must be fined whatever the woman's husband demands and the court allows. But if there is serious injury, you are to take life for life, eye for eye, tooth for tooth, hand for hand, foot for foot, burn for burn, wound for wound, bruise for bruise.
> (Exodus 21:22–25)

RESPECTING LIFE | 93

The idea is that these people are brawling and out of control to such an extent that they are responsible for whatever injury occurs. They may not have meant to hit the pregnant woman, but they did, and they take responsibility for it. The translation of some of the terms is debated, but the point is that any damage to her or her child is to be punished.

This shows that the concern is not only for death, but for any damage to another person's health. We see this explicitly in other laws:

> If people quarrel and one person hits another with a stone or with their fist and the victim does not die but is confined to bed, the one who struck the blow will not be held liable if the other can get up and walk around outside with a staff; however, the guilty party must pay the injured person for any loss of time and see that the victim is completely healed.
>
> (Exodus 21:18–19)

The key idea is the responsibility of the guilty party for any damage he or she has caused.

The Old Testament laws were wise to the variety of circumstances in which murder could take place. A recurring issue in our courts today is that of harming someone who is stealing from you. I tend to think that if people break into my house, they deserve whatever I can throw at them, but there must be an issue of proportional response. Here's how the Old Testament law dealt with it:

> If a thief is caught breaking in at night and is struck a fatal blow, the defender is not guilty of bloodshed; but if it happens after sunrise, the defender is guilty of bloodshed.
>
> (Exodus 22:2–3)

The difference between night-time and daytime probably included a variety of factors. Someone breaking in at night is more threatening, help is less available, and care in fighting is less easy. Also, in the daytime you could see the thief's face and so later on make an appropriate accusation.

Taking responsibility for people

The outworking of this command also includes a broader responsibility for people's lives and health. So if you have a bull which happens to gore someone to death, you are not held responsible. But:

> If, however, the bull has had the habit of goring and the owner has been warned but has not kept it penned up and it kills a man or woman, the bull is to be stoned and its owner also is to be put to death.
>
> (Exodus 21:29)

So if you know what your bull is like, you need to keep it locked up and so keep people safe. You must take responsibility for people's welfare.

Here's a different example:

> When you build a new house, make a parapet around your roof so that you may not bring the guilt of bloodshed on your house if someone falls from the roof.
>
> (Deuteronomy 22:8)

This is the original health and safety instruction! Houses had flat roofs and steps up the side. So the roof was used like a patio. But a roof without a wall round the edge was a real health hazard. So you must take responsibility for your family and your visitors by building that wall.

These Old Testament examples might seem irrelevant to today because few of us own bulls or build our own houses. But we must see the key idea of failing to take responsibility for people's welfare. It is well summed up in this command: 'Do not do anything that endangers your neighbour's life. I am the LORD' (Leviticus 19:16).

The value of life

These prohibitions on murder and injury all point us to the value of life. So we read:

> Whoever sheds human blood,
>   by humans shall their blood be shed;
> for in the image of God
>   has God made mankind.
> (Genesis 9:6)

This is why it's OK to kill a chicken but not a person – the person is made in God's image. People have inherent value, and so life is to be protected. This is where the idea of the 'sanctity of life' comes from. Our life is a sacred thing given by God, and it is not to be taken away by anyone else without just cause.

Of course, the verse above says that anyone who kills will also be killed: murder was a just cause for capital punishment. In the Old Testament, many crimes, including murder, were punished by the taking of the culprit's life.

In each of these cases, there is a concern for appropriate evidence:

> Anyone who kills a person is to be put to death as a murderer only on the testimony of witnesses. But no one is to be put to death on the testimony of only one witness.
> (Numbers 35:30)

This was to protect people from false accusations and wrongful convictions – a key concern also in questions over capital punishment today. These verses do not decide the issue on capital punishment nowadays, because the Old Testament laws were for Israel as a nation state, and we cannot simply transfer them to every nation state today. But it must surely mean that capital punishment is still possible now, rather than always being ruled out of court.

The other occasion where life could be taken justly was in war. This was not considered unjust killing. The area of 'just-war theory' and its application to today is complicated, and also, we must recognize that wars in the Old Testament are not the same as nation states fighting today. But there is some similarity, and I think there is ample evidence that nations can protect themselves through war, and that the sad loss of life that results is not the same as murder.

Not murdering today

What is prohibited so far in these commands?

Murder and manslaughter

It includes what we would call murder – that is, premeditation and intent to kill someone. It also includes what is called voluntary manslaughter, which is when there is intent to kill but not the premeditation, such as killing someone in a rage.

It also includes categories of involuntary manslaughter, that is, where there is no intent to kill but the person is in

RESPECTING LIFE | 97

some way responsible for the death. This can be because of gross negligence, such as not taking appropriate precautions as a climbing instructor. Or it can be because of a dangerous activity, such as reckless driving.

So we must first resist any temptation to do deliberate harm to others. Few of us may be tempted to plan a murder, but it is not beyond any one of us. More of us might have tempers and be in danger of hitting another. We may not plan to kill the individual, but the person's head may hit the kerb as he or she falls over, and the resulting injury or death is our fault. We must respect life, and beware of what will endanger it.

This clearly includes areas like dangerous or drunk driving. It is the thought of what I could possibly do to other people that keeps me below the speed limit and self-aware on the roads. Some of us will have responsibility for areas of health and safety at work or home. I know some health and safety legislation gets silly, but the basic idea is very biblical: if something is dangerous, we must take responsibility for it; we must not endanger people's lives.

Suicide

These laws also apply to suicide. Older descriptions of suicide called it 'self-murder', which is what it is and why it is wrong.

This is a desperately painful area, for at least two reasons. First, those considering suicide feel so utterly awful to be doing it at all. They feel as if life is not worth living; death feels like an escape; they do not think they can go on as they are. It has been said that suicide is a very selfish act, because in doing it you are only thinking about yourself. That is true, but we must also recognize that it is the selfish act of a person who cannot see an alternative. It is often connected to depression, and the blackness can simply feel overwhelming.

This means we must both say that it is wrong and we must sympathize deeply with those tempted by it.

This is also a painful area because most people end up knowing someone who commits suicide. How should we consider the person's death, especially if he or she was a Christian? Some people are aware of the Roman Catholic teaching that suicide is a 'mortal sin', which means that the person forfeits his or her salvation. I do not think that is true. It is a sin, and it means ending our life with a sinful act, but that act can be forgiven just as much as any other can.

Assisted suicide

This command also applies to assisted suicide. As I write this, the Assisted Dying Bill in the UK has recently been defeated in Parliament. But it is probably only a matter of time before assisted suicide is made legal, as it already is in a number of European countries and a number of US states. In the meantime, anyone in the UK wanting to die can use the services of the now unfortunately well-known Swiss company, Dignitas. They say they work for the worldwide implementation of the last human right – the right to die.

Usually, the argument is that the person's quality of life is so poor that life is not worth living. It is true that life can be appalling, and we must be so sympathetic to that. But we need God to tell us what is and isn't worthwhile. And while God decides to give life, that life is worth living.

People also say we should have a right to end our lives if we wish to. That means wanting the right to choose how and when we die. But Christians will always want to acknowledge God's sovereignty over their lives and death and submit to him.

People argue that they want to be able to die with dignity (and this is where Dignitas gets its name). But dignity needs to be defined. It is being made in God's image that gives each of us dignity, and while we are made in his image, we retain that dignity whatever our health. I think God would say that being put to death is a great indignity indeed.

So we must continue to say that deliberately ending someone's life is wrong.

Again, we must be full of sympathy for people's suffering. This can be a desperately tricky area. But such suffering does not justify killing.

We should be clear that the decision to end life deliberately in assisted suicide is different from withdrawing treatment, and so allowing someone to die naturally. It is also different from what's called 'double effect' where you know that pain relief may also hasten death. In this case, it is reasonable to give appropriate medication to relieve pain – it is being given for that purpose and not to kill – even though you know the effect that it will have.

It is the respect for life that has motivated Christians in the past to start hospices to care for the terminally ill. In fact, it is countries that have continued to prohibit assisted dying that have the most developed hospice movements. So as well as expressing our disagreement and dismay at assisted dying, we must also support the care of those who are dying, treating them with respect and dignity for as long as God gives them life.

Abortion

The other huge area that we need to consider is abortion or the termination of pregnancy (I'll use both terms). Once again we are walking on very sensitive ground, and dealing with a variety of situations. Some will have had abortions and feel crippled by guilt. Some may have been pressured into it, feeling they had little choice in the matter. Others may have made a free choice and not considered they have done anything wrong. Meanwhile, the men in the equation are rarely to be seen. It is emotive and difficult, but we have to deal with it.

The issue we have to wrestle with here is this: when does life begin? If life only begins at birth, then terminating a pregnancy is not murder because there is no life to kill. But such a position is not sustainable. No one can claim that the baby is more alive just for being out of the womb. Life clearly does not start at birth – as a pregnant mother will testify; her baby is alive and kicking well before that.

This is shown practically in that a foetus often lives outside the womb from twenty-four weeks or so, and hence the current legislation in the UK is that terminations are only allowed up to that time, unless there are other factors.

So when does life start? The legislation focuses on when life is sustainable outside the womb. But that is a different question. Just because a baby would not survive outside the womb does not mean it is less of a life.

This leads us back to life beginning at the moment of conception. Certainly, the biblical picture is of unborn children being seen as truly human and alive. We saw that in the case of the pregnant woman being injured above (Exodus 21:22–25). It is also seen when David describes God knowing him in the womb:

For you created my inmost being;
　　you knit me together in my mother's womb.
I praise you because I am fearfully and wonderfully made;
　　your works are wonderful,
　　I know that full well.
My frame was not hidden from you
　　when I was made in the secret place,
　　when I was woven together in the depths of the earth.

Your eyes saw my unformed body;
    all the days ordained for me were written in your book
    before one of them came to be.
(Psalm 139:13–16)

Life begins at conception, and so I believe the clear position of the Bible is that abortion is murder.

This has been recognized in medical circles from the time of the Hippocratic Oath in the fifth century BC, which included this phrase: 'I will not give to a woman a pessary to procure abortion.' That positon was maintained until the second half of the twentieth century. In the UK, it changed with the Abortion Act of 1967. That Act did not intend to result in abortion on demand, but that is effectively what has happened. The result is that in England and Wales there are currently around 185,000 terminations each year.

Terminations in exceptional cases

There are, of course, many situations where abortion seems more reasonable. Some say it should be allowed where there is a severe abnormality in the child, although we should note that this reason currently accounts for only about 1% of terminations. Allowing it there, though, says that a disabled life is not as valuable as an able-bodied one. Biblically, we'd say that the value of our life comes from being created in God's image and is not connected to how able-bodied we are.

Some say abortion should be allowed in a difficult family situation where coping with another child seems unfeasible. I sympathize hugely with those who feel overwhelmed with that sort of situation. But avoiding difficult consequences isn't a reason to do something that is wrong.

Pregnancy following rape is probably the worst-case scenario. I can't even begin to imagine how difficult that must be. But I still can't see it justifying what God says is wrong. My hope would be that all women who end up pregnant and who do not want the child would consider giving that child up for adoption, and so honouring its life rather than ending it.

We must pause for a moment here to speak to those who have had an abortion and who consequently feel guilty. I have known people in that situation. Please recognize that God understood whatever situation you were in. That doesn't make it OK, but he does understand what you felt. Please know that he offers forgiveness, full and free, and all you need to do is ask. If you've not done so before, please speak to someone about what you've been through. It can feel shaming, and some churches can feel like the last place you'd want to speak about it. But talking, sharing and praying with others is part of how God will help you.

In all these ways, we are called to not murder, but rather to respect life today.

The call to love rather than hate

The call not to murder can be applied even more fully though. Jesus not only repeats the command, but reapplies it to our hearts. Here's what he says:

> You have heard that it was said to the people long ago, 'You shall not murder, and anyone who murders will be subject to judgment.' But I tell you that anyone who is angry with a brother or sister will be subject to judgment. Again, anyone who says to a brother or sister, 'Raca,' is answerable to the court. And anyone who says, 'You fool!' will be in danger of the fire of hell.
> (Matthew 5:21–22)

Jesus goes beyond the action prohibited – murdering – to the heart attitude of hatred. It is hatred in its different forms that leads people to murder, whether through bitterness or revenge or envy. Such hatred was also prohibited in the Old Testament (see Leviticus 19:16–17).

The call of 'Raca' is an Aramaic word of contempt. Saying 'You fool' is not simply saying, 'You're an idiot', but it is expressing malice towards someone. So Jesus is moving from anger in the heart to the way it is expressed in our words and treatment of people. He is concerned with our attitude towards others: is it murderous? Is it one of hatred, contempt or hostility?

Jesus goes on in Matthew 5 to speak about the importance of being reconciled to people. So Jesus is not just against hatred but, more positively, wants people to be at peace in their relationships. He knows that there will be those who annoy us, irritate us and hurt us. Rather than letting that boil up into hatred, we seek reconciliation.

John makes the same equation between hatred and murder: 'Anyone who hates a brother or sister is a murderer, and you know that no murderer has eternal life residing in him' (1 John 3:15).

In this passage John not only warns us against hatred; he also defines hatred as the opposite of love, and calls us to love rather than hate. Remember that Jesus' summary of the law included loving our neighbour as ourselves (Mark 12:31; cf. Leviticus 19:18).

We are also reminded of Paul's call:

> Do not repay anyone evil for evil. Be careful to do what is right in the eyes of everyone. If it is possible, as far as it depends on you, live at peace with everyone. Do not take revenge, my dear friends, but leave room for God's wrath,

for it is written: 'It is mine to avenge; I will repay,' says
the Lord.
(Romans 12:17–19)

So the command not to murder has now developed into
something much more far-reaching. Our respect for people
and their lives means seeking reconciliation and peace in
relationships, looking to love rather than hate, and a gentle
response to provocation.

Responding to God

We need to be honest with ourselves here. We need honesty
in areas that result in actual physical harm to others. We listed
some earlier: negligence in industry, dangerous driving,
abortion, hitting someone in anger. Have we done, or do we
do, these things? Do we show respect for life, or disregard?

We need honesty over our attitudes as well. We may think
we'd never 'murder', but actually we murder every day in our
hearts. We can nurture angry and bitter thoughts towards
people. We can daydream of moments of vengeance. We can
betray attitudes of racism, sexism and classism, and others
where we condemn entire groups of people. We can be those
who stir up dissension rather than promoting peace. And we
can certainly fail to love those around us. In all these ways and
more, we 'murder'.

So we need to be honest and then confess. And then celebrate
the work of the Lord Jesus who kept this command perfectly. He
respected every life he met, and never endangered anyone.
He was only ever rightly angry, and he was always loving. And
he gives his righteousness to us, and dies for all our 'murders'.

So we celebrate salvation, and we ask for strength and help
to live as we should.

7. FAITHFUL MARRIAGE

Sex and marriage. They used to be joined together, at least vaguely, but that was lost a long time ago. But even with the connection between sex and marriage undone, there was still at least some respect for marriage and some concept of loyalty within it. Committing adultery was frowned upon.

But things have changed, and our culture is confused.

Marriage is still viewed warmly by many. A wedding day is celebrated as a romantic ideal. A golden wedding anniversary is honoured by everyone. Many people like the idea of being married.

And yet marriage is constantly derided as an outdated institution. It is seen as restrictive and limiting. Unfaithfulness in marriage is rarely smiled at, but more often accepted as normal. There are websites available specifically for married people to find others who want to commit adultery. One tag line reads: 'Life is short. Have an affair.' The implication: life in a faithful marriage is boring and wasted.

A recent newspaper article on the topic was entitled: 'Faithful at 50? Dream on.'[3] Its argument was that infidelity should be regarded as normal rather than exceptional. It reported that roughly half of women and 65% of men were unfaithful in marriage before they reached forty. So is faithful marriage good or bad? We're confused.

Currently 42% of marriages end in divorce. The divorce rate hasn't been rising particularly, but that is probably because of the increasing number of people who decide never to get married at all, and hence, if their relationship ends, it's never recorded.

Most recently, marriage has been in the headlines because of same-sex marriage. The media has often held up marriage as a wonderful thing for people to aspire to – 'If two people love each other and want to commit to each other for life, then no one should stop them.' It has also seen marriage as a plastic thing that can be reshaped as we wish. If its basis is purely people's love and commitment, then why only have two people, why have age restrictions, and so on? Still more confusion.

Meanwhile, most of society goes on having sex outside marriage. We're told that it's a physical activity only for pleasure – 'It's just sex.' But elsewhere we're told that it gives us meaning and brings intimacy in relationships – it's never *just* sex. People want freedom in sex *and* closeness in relationships. And so we show our confusion.

Sexual activity is starting younger; there is more sex education and advice than ever; and people have more sexual freedom, and yet the result doesn't seem to be satisfaction and healthiness, but more and more hurt.

What a mess!

All of which makes the seventh commandment seem both hopelessly outdated and amazingly relevant: 'You shall not commit adultery' (Exodus 20:14).

Remember these are good laws

Have you heard the joke about Moses coming down to the Israelites and saying, 'I've got good news and bad news. The good news is I've got him down to ten; the bad news is that adultery is still in.'

Jokes like that see God's commands as being unhelpfully restrictive. They hold us back from what would otherwise be fun. That is most true of our views on sex. In this, above all areas of life, we can easily think that God is a killjoy. Sex is a universal and powerful urge, and we easily feel the 'need' to express it.

The truth of course is the opposite way round. As we said in our opening chapter, God knows what is best for us because he is our Creator. And he wants what's best for us because he is our Saviour.

His commands are for our good, for our protection and for our flourishing, not for our limitation. Let's remember that as we explore this command together.

Faithfulness in marriage

This command is first of all for faithfulness in marriage.

We learn about marriage in the very first chapters of the Bible. God creates man and woman as wonderfully complementary and suitable for each other. We read: 'That is why a man leaves his father and mother and is united to his wife, and they become one flesh' (Genesis 2:24).

In marriage, a new family unit is formed. Parents are left behind (although still 'honoured' – see chapter 5), and husband and wife are 'united'. They are bound together. So much so that they become 'one flesh'; they are welded together into a new whole.

Sometimes people will say to someone about their spouse, 'Where's your other half?' They are probably speaking better than they know, because that is what married people are now: two halves of a new whole. They haven't simply entered into a new arrangement; they've become part of each other. They haven't simply taken their relationship to a higher level of commitment, but moved to a different type of existence.

When Jesus is discussing marriage, he quotes this verse from Genesis and goes on to say, 'Therefore what God has joined together, let no one separate' (Matthew 19:6).

Jesus is saying that God is the one who has joined husband and wife together. He has fused them. So if God is behind their 'one-fleshness', then no one had better separate them. They would be undoing God's work.

This sketches out for us what marriage is: it is a union of a man and woman in an exclusive relationship of lifelong faithfulness.

And that is what marriage should be, but it is well recognized in the Bible that it doesn't always happen in practice – people break marriages. They *do* separate what God has joined together. And that is most commonly done through adultery.

Sex is designed by God for the exclusive setting of marriage, where it both wonderfully pictures and aids the unity of a marriage. And so adultery, sexual intimacy with someone else, is a terrible act of unfaithfulness.

So in this command God is calling his people to faithfulness in marriage. He is saying in no uncertain terms, stay committed to your wife or husband; don't go looking elsewhere; guard your affections, and keep them only for your spouse.

We've commented on the mixed views of marriage around today, but for many people unfaithfulness in marriage is simply accepted. Some cultures have presumed that husbands would have a mistress, and, sometimes, that wives would have a lover. A recent book actually argues that if marriages are to last, we have to expect infidelity! In others words, marriage needs that sort of flexibility if it's not to break. This sees marriage as a nice idea, but too limiting, so couples need an outlet. However, it says nothing about the shattering effects that unfaithfulness has on a marriage.

By contrast, God's design is for complete loyalty and faithfulness: that is what makes marriage what it is. It is only with the walls of faithfulness in place that there can be true freedom in a relationship: freedom to be open and intimate, freedom to trust and depend. God knew what he was doing in designing marriage and saying that it needs faithfulness.

Faithfulness in practice

As with the other commandments, we see this one worked out in practice in the detailed, situational laws of the Old Testament. So we read:

> If a man commits adultery with another man's wife – with the wife of his neighbour – both the adulterer and the adulteress are to be put to death.
> (Leviticus 20:10)

> If a man is found sleeping with another man's wife, both the man who slept with her and the woman must die. You must purge the evil from Israel.
> (Deuteronomy 22:22)

God took this very seriously indeed. Adultery was going against how he has joined people together, and destroying marriages and families.

But as well as warnings against adultery, there were also calls to faithfulness and delight in marriage:

> Drink water from your own cistern,
>   running water from your own well.
> Should your springs overflow in the streets,
>   your streams of water in the public squares?
> Let them be yours alone,
>   never to be shared with strangers.
> May your fountain be blessed,
>   and may you rejoice in the wife of your youth.
> A loving doe, a graceful deer –
>   may her breasts satisfy you always,
>   may you ever be intoxicated with her love.
> Why, my son, be intoxicated with another man's wife?
>   Why embrace the bosom of a wayward woman?
> (Proverbs 5:15–20)

Here is a call to sexual exclusiveness: only drink from your own cistern, that is, only have sex with your wife. But as well as the call to exclusivity, there is a call to delight and enjoyment. May you rejoice in your wife; may you be satisfied with her body; may you be intoxicated with her love.

The Bible is not embarrassed about the delights of love and the enjoyment of sex. God thinks that sex is fantastic – it's just got to be with your spouse.

Sexual purity

This call to faithfulness in marriage links with a more general call to sexual purity. I'm aware as soon as I use the term that it can have negative overtones. 'Purity' doesn't sound appealing. But by 'sexual purity' I simply mean using sex as God intends, and so viewing and using it rightly and lovingly.

If you are married, then sexual purity means being faithful to your wife or husband. But what if you're not married? Strictly speaking, you need to be married to be able to commit adultery – so does this command not apply to single people?

Yes, it does. Other laws in the Old Testament show that sex outside of marriage is wrong. And that becomes even clearer in the New Testament. We saw that when Jesus quotes some of the Ten Commandments, he expands on them. When he mentions 'adultery', he adds 'sexual immorality' (Matthew 15:19). Sexual immorality is a wider category than adultery, but Jesus thinks it's implied by the command.

Sexual immorality is really the opposite of sexual purity; it is using sex in a way that God does not intend or want. That includes sexual activity outside marriage, and sex with someone of the same sex, even if you are legally married.

And we can go further than actions: Jesus says,

> You have heard that it was said, 'You shall not commit adultery.'
> But I tell you that anyone who looks at a woman lustfully has
> already committed adultery with her in his heart.
> (Matthew 5:27–28)

Lust here is the imagining of sex with someone to whom I am not married. It doesn't mean we can't notice that someone is attractive; it moves on to picturing sexual activity that, if realized, would count as adultery.

This includes pornography, which is looking at physical images lustfully. It includes fantasy, which is looking at mental images lustfully. I think it must also include romantic or emotional fantasy too, that is, where you don't necessarily imagine having sex with someone you're not married to, but you do imagine intimacy or romance with him or her.

It's a generalization, but often men tend to be tempted more by visual images, physical or mental, whereas women tend to be tempted more by romantic fantasies. But for all of us, whoever we are, whatever we are tempted by, the command not to commit adultery means both faithfulness in our marriage and sexual purity more generally.

Flee from temptation

I want to apply this negatively and positively. The apostle Paul says, 'Flee from sexual immorality' (1 Corinthians 6:18).

It is a simple command: run away from any wrong use of sex.

When you see sexual immorality looming on the horizon, you need to turn around and head in the opposite direction. Telling us to 'flee' in this way is significant. It means sexual immorality is not something to be trifled with or dabbled in.

That is true of all sin, but especially true of sexual sin, because of the power of temptation. If you let yourself get too close, you can get sucked in. Like a magnet and metal, the closer together they get, the stronger the pull. So too with sexual sin. The answer is to turn around and run early on.

Attraction to people

So what does that mean in practice? It means that if we're aware of an attraction to someone we're not married to, someone whom we shouldn't pursue a relationship with, we take action. That might entail telling our spouse, or, if we're not married, a trusted friend. We tell someone both to get it out into the open and to make ourselves accountable. It will mean we will be careful in our contact with that person, not spending too long in his or her company, especially alone.

We need to be realistic here. It would be strange if each of us went through life and the only person we ever found attractive was our spouse. That would be lovely, but it would also be very unusual. And yet, too often Christians seem surprised when an attraction to someone else springs up. We shouldn't be surprised – it's going to happen. The only question is: what will we do when we become aware of it? Will we flee?

You will probably know, as I do, stories of married people who ended up having an affair with someone at work or at church. They are always sad stories. They never have happy endings – even if the wonderful grace of forgiveness and restoration can be applied. But these people would not have ended up where they did if they had told their spouses they found those others attractive early on and had avoided contact with them.

Pornography

This command means that if pornography is an issue for us, we must take action. Again, telling someone else is a great first step. If you are married, you should tell your spouse. Confess your sin and ask for forgiveness, because you are breaking your marriage vows. Speaking to someone else as well is usually very useful – a good friend or a church leader. They can advise, ask appropriate questions and keep you accountable.

Practical action can help as well. One friend of mine doesn't have a TV because of the temptation to watch what he shouldn't. Another friend doesn't have internet access in his study. Another friend has his wife set the password on the cable TV because of the channels he could otherwise access. Various internet programs and blocks can help too.

Whatever you do, don't just let it carry on. Don't convince yourself that it's under control when it keeps happening.

Flee!

Being careful

This also means we are careful with our eyes and how we look at other people. Job says he has made a covenant with his eyes not to look at a woman lustfully (Job 31:1). It is not easy or even possible to stop images or ideas appearing in our heads, but we can either banish them or indulge them.

This means we are careful with romantic or emotional fantasies as well as physical ones. It might mean being careful with the sort of literature we read, either because of descriptions of sex, or because it fosters thoughts of escapist romance.

We need to beware of temptation – we need to run away.

Speaking and confessing

A key part of this is speaking to someone else about where we are tempted or where we are failing. That is usually a spouse, a friend, or both. Speaking and confessing like this is so important, because sin loves the darkness. It festers and grows in the dark. But when we tell someone, we bring it out into the light and often this already causes it to start to wither.

This is especially true if you are married. Yes, it is true for everyone, but I have seen too many marriages where this didn't happen when it should have done. Here's the lesson: confess before you are caught!

Confessing is the right thing to do because we have sinned against someone. But it is also the best thing to do because it shows that we are serious and that we want to change. It shows your spouse that you want him or her to be able to trust you. I know it is a painful first step, but it is a first step in the right direction, and it is better than any alternative.

Let me add a word to those who might find a spouse confessing to something. First, recognize the hurt that unfaithfulness causes; don't be tempted to say that your husband looking at pornography doesn't matter just because it's so common. It *does* matter and it *does* hurt. And the greater the unfaithfulness, the greater the hurt. But also recognize that we are all sexual sinners in different ways. Beware of self-righteousness.

Second, try to honour the confession. Your spouse wants to come clean, he or she wants to change, and wants your forgiveness. That can take time to work through and it isn't always easy. But this is where the wonderful dynamics of the gospel are seen: confession, asking for forgiveness; forgiveness being given and accepted. We are to forgive each other as Christ forgave us (Colossians 3:13). That can take a long time, and even when forgiveness is given, trust may not yet be regained. But God's grace allows us to forgive and for relationships to be restored.

Honour marriage

We've seen the negative application: flee sexual immorality. Now here's the positive: honour marriage. The letter to the Hebrews says this: 'Marriage should be honoured by all, and the marriage bed kept pure, for God will judge the adulterer and all the sexually immoral' (Hebrews 13:4).

Marriage should be honoured by all. That means everyone reading this – single, married, divorced, widowed or whatever – everyone is to honour marriage.

We will do that by faithfulness in our own marriages. But we will also do it in the way we view and speak about marriage. If we honour marriage, then we will hold it in high esteem; we will think of it as a precious thing; we will speak well of it. We will always want to say things that support marriage in general, and specific marriages in particular. We will hate saying something that would undermine marriage. And we will want to act in a way that will honour rather than endanger marriages.

We desperately need that honouring of marriage in our culture. We saw at the start that our culture has mixed views on marriage, but overall it does marriage down rather than building it up. There are moments when marriage is spoken well of, but it is a very occasional, only very small voice.

Just think: when was the last song or film or novel that celebrated lifelong faithful marriage? I can't even think of one. But there's a continual stream of songs, films and novels that say that faithful marriage is boring. Virtually every mention of sex in films or books is outside marriage.

So we need to respond, especially within our churches, by honouring marriage, saying that lifelong, faithful, committed marriage is a good and beautiful thing.

I want to say to my wife, 'I long to stay faithful to you and grow old with you, and that is the most fantastic future imaginable.' That's what I want to say, rather than looking over my wife's shoulder wondering what might have been or who else there might be. I want every married person to say such things, and beware of wrong things. And I want every unmarried person to want that, pray for that and encourage that in all the marriages they know.

This also means that couples and churches should invest in marriage. We know that marriages need to be worked at. Simple things like guarding good time together, arranging dates and making sure there's time for sex are really important. You may be surprised by the mention of time for sex, but it's true. As a pastor, I end up warning single people against having sex and encouraging married couples to have more sex! The fact is that within the busyness of life, tiredness from work and pressure of children, sex can often be sidelined. It might not sound romantic, but scheduling time, going to bed early and discussing when sex might happen are all healthy and helpful parts of marriage.

Within churches we honour marriage by preparing couples for marriage and then supporting them within it. That may mean running occasional courses, but it also means offering a safe enough place to say that you're having difficulties. We need to be honest here and say that not every marriage runs smoothly and most marriages have rough patches. We need to be able to talk, encourage and support at such times.

And so we will honour marriage, and keep the marriage bed pure.

Responding to God

It is unusual to speak about sexual sin like this without people feeling guilty. Most of us will have been reminded of actions and thoughts of the past, and convicted about thoughts and actions of the present. Where do we go with that guilt?

As with all these commands, we go first to Jesus who kept this command perfectly. He never committed adultery, he never looked at a woman lustfully and he always honoured marriage. He lived the life that we should have lived. And then he died the death we should have died for our sins, including all our sexual sins.

So we go to Jesus and we rejoice in forgiveness.

But second, we press on knowing there can be change. Paul writes to the church in Corinth and refers to the sexually immoral, adulterers, those engaging in homosexual acts, and so on. And then he says,

> And that is what some of you were. But you were washed, you
> were sanctified, you were justified in the name of the Lord Jesus
> Christ and by the Spirit of our God.
> (1 Corinthians 6:11)

We have been washed clean of such sin. And there can be
change.

I often tell people that we will fight for sexual purity for the
rest of our lives. It's not a battle that you win and then the
battle is over. But the battle lines can move. We can win in
such a way as to make progress, so that what we were tempted
by before is less of an issue now. It is not hopeless.

This is, of course, true of all sin, but with sexual sin we
often need to hear and know that a little more. Do not commit
adultery; flee from sexual immorality; honour marriage.

8. RECOGNIZING OWNERSHIP

I live in north Cambridge. Now, it's not the most sought-after area in the city, but it's perfectly pleasant. However, in an average month there are over 100 thefts within one mile of where our church meets. That's almost four a day. The most common are shoplifting, robbery and burglary. The most common item to be stolen across Cambridge is bicycles – this is a cycling city. There are around 3,000 bike thefts each year – that's nearly ten a day.

Recently several BT repair vans were seen in a local road. Workers were lifting up manhole covers and doing whatever they do to telephone and internet cables. Except that they weren't. They weren't BT employees at all. What they were doing was stripping the cables for the copper, which they would go on to sell.

One of the biggest areas of rising theft is online. Someone at church recently had two incidents at work: one of credit card theft and one of online hacking resulting in the transfer of money out of an account. Across the whole UK identity theft, card fraud and similar now total over a million pounds a day.

Just consider some of the normal things we do every day because of the prevalence of theft:

- we lock our front doors;
- we lock our cars and bikes;
- we use pin codes on our cards;
- we have etching or security tags on valuable items;
- we need passwords online;
- we use codes or identity markers for our phones, computers and tablets.

All this makes God's law seem very relevant and very sensible: 'You shall not steal' (Exodus 20:15).

Understanding ownership

Each of the Ten Commandments has a certain background. 'Do not murder' is set against the value of life; 'Do not commit adultery' has the background of marriage.

What background is being assumed here?

It is the belief in ownership. That there is such a thing as personal property, so that what is yours is yours, and what is mine is mine.

The wider background is that of working and earning. God has made a productive world in which we have resources and skills, and the energy and time to use them. And so God expects us to grow food, or provide services, or work for others. As a result, we will earn money or grow crops; we will build or buy houses; we will put food in our cupboards and clothes in our wardrobes; we will buy toys for our children, and more. And our money and our possessions are ours.

It is, of course, true that everything we have is ultimately God's. He is the great 'owner' of all creation (1 Chronicles 29:11–12). That shapes how we view what we own, and how we use what we own, but the fact remains that it is regarded as our own.

The point is that the Bible doesn't support a communal view of living where everything belongs to everyone else. Rather, there is private as well as public property. We are going to learn about giving away what we own, and sharing what we own, but we begin with ownership itself.

Respecting ownership

This command is first a call to respect ownership, to respect the fact that someone's mobile phone, bike, book or whatever else is theirs and not mine, and so not to steal it.

I remember the first time that I was ever stolen from. I was at university and someone went into my room in a hall of residence and stole my wallet. (I was in the shower at the time.) At first, I couldn't believe it, then I was annoyed but kind of amused, and then, as the practical results of losing cards and money sank in, I was angry. That's the most common reaction to theft, and it's the right one. We are angry because ownership should be respected.

Later laws unpack this simple principle in more detail. We begin with the worst form of stealing: 'Anyone who kidnaps someone is to be put to death, whether the victim has been sold or is still in the kidnapper's possession' (Exodus 21:16).

The word for 'kidnap' here is the same as in the eighth commandment: this is anyone who 'steals' a person. The severe punishment shows the value of people. You don't get put to death if you steal a sheep, but you do if you steal a person.

We can immediately think of the modern-day trafficking of people. These individuals are either kidnapped, tricked or coerced into some form of slavery. And God tells us that this is an appalling thing.

There is to be no stealing of people, and there is to be no stealing of possessions either:

> Anyone who steals must certainly make restitution, but if they have nothing, they must be sold to pay for their theft. If the stolen animal is found alive in their possession – whether ox or donkey or sheep – they must pay back double.
> (Exodus 22:3–4)

This tells us both that stealing an animal was wrong, and that there was to be restitution for the theft and punishment of the crime. The thief had to give back what was stolen plus another one. If all he had to do was give back the animal, then he would end up no worse off than when he started; the extra animal is a 'fine' to dissuade people from stealing. If they do steal and they are caught, they will end up one animal down, rather than one animal up.

But the command goes wider than just straight stealing. You mustn't do anything that damages other people's personal property. For example:

> If anyone grazes their livestock in a field or vineyard and lets them stray and they graze in someone else's field, the offender must make restitution from the best of their own field or vineyard.
> (Exodus 22:5)

So I shouldn't benefit from your grass or grapes. Today we might say I shouldn't benefit from my neighbour's Wi-Fi. Also, I shouldn't cause any damage to your property:

If a fire breaks out and spreads into thorn-bushes so that it burns
sheaves of corn or standing corn or the whole field, the one who
started the fire must make restitution.
(Exodus 22:6)

If anyone uncovers a pit or digs one and fails to cover it and an
ox or a donkey falls into it, the one who opened the pit must pay
the owner for the loss and take the dead animal in exchange.
(Exodus 21:33)

If I do something that causes damage to your property, then
I am responsible. You shouldn't suffer the loss of your possessions because of me. And that is the case whatever my
motivation.

I remember an example of this in our family. Walking back
from the park, one of our kids knocked a bike against a parked
car which resulted in a scratch on the paintwork. It wasn't
a very big scratch, but it was clearly there and clearly done
by us.

So we had done something that damaged someone else's
property. The temptation just to keep walking down the street
was high. The justifications of 'We didn't mean to do it'; 'It's
only small'; 'This sort of thing happens all the time' ran round
in my head. But my wife rightly said we should leave a note
apologizing and that we would pay. The owner of the car then
got in touch and said, 'It's only small; don't worry about it.'
But he also said he was amazed that we'd offered.

There are also laws about what happens if you give
something to me for safekeeping, or borrow from someone.
For example:

If anyone borrows an animal from their neighbour and it is
injured or dies while the owner is not present, they must make

restitution. But if the owner is with the animal, the borrower will not have to pay. If the animal was hired, the money paid for the hire covers the loss.

(Exodus 22:14–15)

So if I borrow my neighbour's drill to do some DIY and it breaks, I should buy him a new one. But not if he is with me at the time, presumably because he can make sure I don't misuse it. And if I hire a drill from a shop, then the breakage is the shop's issue.

It's not that we should apply all these details precisely. That's partly because of differences in circumstances between then and today. Also, as we have said before, these laws are examples of the principle in practice, and even in Israel they would have had to think through each case separately. But we should see the point very clearly: we respect people's ownership. So we do nothing to damage what belongs to others, and we make recompense if we do.

The laws go further than property though. They include anything that we might 'owe' someone.

Do not defraud or rob your neighbour.
Do not hold back the wages of a hired worker overnight.
(Leviticus 19:13)

Stealing is not only taking something that doesn't belong to you; it's also not paying something you owe someone. If I don't pay your wages, then I've stolen from you. This can then be broadened to honesty in business generally. For example:

Do not use dishonest standards when measuring length, weight or quantity. Use honest scales and honest weights, an honest

RECOGNIZING OWNERSHIP | 125

ephah and an honest hin. I am the LORD your God, who brought
you out of Egypt.
(Leviticus 19:35)

Any form of dishonesty that leaves people out of pocket is a
form of stealing.

Lastly, this respect for ownership also means that I take
responsibility to help look after your property:

> If you see your fellow Israelite's ox or sheep straying, do not
> ignore it but be sure to take it back to its owner. If they do not
> live near you or if you do not know who owns it, take it home
> with you and keep it until they come looking for it. Then give it
> back. Do the same if you find their donkey or cloak or anything
> else they have lost. Do not ignore it.
> (Deuteronomy 22:1–3)

Here it's not your fault that your neighbour's animals are
wandering the streets or that he or she dropped a coat. But if
you come across it, you should take responsibility for it. So
when we find someone's mobile phone on the train, we hand
it in or try to return it. We don't keep it, or even just leave it
there. Rather, we respect other people's ownership.

Respecting ownership today

I've mentioned some applications in the last section, but let's
think through some more.

This commandment must mean we are concerned about
modern-day slavery, which is one of the hidden evils of our
society. It lies behind much of the sex industry, and some of
the clothing and food industries too. We should be very glad
of efforts like the Modern Slavery Bill in the UK. We should

do what we can to support organizations that work in this area and campaign in other ways.

We should be careful not to steal in the straightforward ways of taking what is not ours. I expect relatively few of us would ever think about robbing someone or shoplifting, but such temptations are not beneath us. Given the right set of circumstances, we could easily do it.

We are probably more tempted where the 'stealing' is less obvious. One of the most common ways is stealing from employers. It can be tiny amounts, like taking envelopes or doing photocopying at work. But without the employer's permission to do so, it is still stealing. We don't consider it like that because we think stealing from an organization or a business is different from stealing from an individual. We can even start to think that our company owes us such things. But it remains stealing nonetheless.

There's also an implication here for working the hours we're contracted to work. For many people that won't be an issue – you probably need to work less than you do, not more – but for some, it really is.

Wasting time at work on social media or not being at work (pulling a 'sickie') or leaving early are all forms of stealing from your employer. Imagine you employed someone to do painting on your house and you paid for ten hours' work, but then discovered he or she had done only six. How would you feel? Rightly, you'd feel angry because the person had deceived you and so stolen from you. But the issues remain the same if we are working for a large company and on a permanent contract.

Another common area today is illegal downloads of music or films. This is, again, simply stealing. The apostle Paul says, 'Give to everyone what you owe them: if you owe taxes, pay taxes; if revenue, then revenue' (Romans 13:7).

I know someone who works as a freelance music teacher and someone else who does handiwork on people's houses. Both of them have to chase people to pay their bills. If they didn't, people simply wouldn't pay for the lessons their children have had or the work they have had done, which would of course be stealing.

I used to be involved in running a training course in Christian ministry where our administrator had to chase people to pay fees. In at least one case she gave up, and the person never paid. They had stolen from us. I'm sure that's not what they believed they were doing, but that is what was happening nonetheless. Let's make sure that's not us.

Another common area is borrowing from people. Studying this subject leads me to make a confession. I borrowed a book from someone many years ago. I had it for a few months, and then the person I'd borrowed it from was returning home to Australia. It was a very useful book and an expensive one too. And I didn't return it to him before he left.

It was partly forgetfulness, but I have to tell you that this thought went through my mind: 'If I don't give it back and he leaves, I'll get to keep it.' That's terrible, isn't it? It is, in fact, stealing. So I wrote to him and apologized, and offered Amazon vouchers as restitution. He very kindly forgave me.

Our church meets in a school hall each week. We have occasionally broken objects: a mug, a display stand, a flip chart. It's very easy just to ignore such things; they'll get lost in the busyness of school life. But that would be a form of stealing too. So we report every breakage and offer to pay for it. We respect that it is the school's property. The result is that the school principal has told me he knows they can trust us.

In all these ways and more, we must avoid stealing.

Being generous

So we must respect ownership. But we can go a step further. With each of the Ten Commandments there is both a negative to avoid and a positive to embrace. So we've seen how we avoid murder, but we promote life. We avoid adultery, but we honour marriage.

So what's the opposite of stealing?

As well as respecting ownership, we are to be generous.

This was seen in the Old Testament in various laws that helped the poor. For example, you were allowed to pick at your neighbour's crops for something to eat, as long as you didn't start to harvest them:

> If you enter your neighbour's vineyard, you may eat all the grapes you want, but do not put any in your basket. If you enter your neighbour's cornfield, you may pick the ears with your hands, but you must not put a sickle to their standing corn.
> (Deuteronomy 23:24–25)

This is a form of welfare for those who didn't have enough. And in the case of the person who owned the vineyard or cornfield, although those grapes and that corn were yours, you were to be generous in giving people access to them.

In addition, you weren't to harvest everything from your fields, so that some was left for the poor:

> When you are harvesting in your field and you overlook a sheaf, do not go back to get it. Leave it for the foreigner, the fatherless and the widow, so that the LORD your God may bless you in all the work of your hands. When you beat the olives from your trees, do not go over the branches a second time. Leave what

remains for the foreigner, the fatherless and the widow. When you harvest the grapes in your vineyard, do not go over the vines again. Leave what remains for the foreigner, the fatherless and the widow. Remember that you were slaves in Egypt. That is why I command you to do this.
(Deuteronomy 24:19–22)

So even though everything in the field was yours, this was a form of enforced generosity. Notice the motivation given: you were slaves, but God rescued you. His kindness to you results in your kindness to others.

There is also the straightforward command to give to those in need:

If anyone is poor among your fellow Israelites in any of the towns of the land that the LORD your God is giving you, do not be hard-hearted or tight-fisted towards them. Rather, be open-handed and freely lend them whatever they need.
(Deuteronomy 15:7–8)

This is exactly the type of generosity that we then see encouraged in the New Testament. Here's a verse from the apostle Paul:

Anyone who has been stealing must steal no longer, but must work, doing something useful with their own hands, that they may have something to share with those in need.
(Ephesians 4:28)

The opposite of stealing here is first of all work. You earn your keep rather than stealing it from others. But Paul doesn't stop there. You now have money and possessions of your own, and so you have things you can share with others. So rather than taking from others, you give to others; rather than stealing, you are generous.

This is where there is a fundamental change of outlook for the Christian. Why am I tempted to steal in all its subtle and not-so-subtle forms? It's because I want things without paying for them. I see the book I've borrowed, or the phone I've found, or the download I could have, and I think, 'I can have that and not pay.' It is fundamentally selfish. It is bettering my life, making me more comfortable, enjoying what I want, at the expense of others.

But for the Christian, life is turned inside out. Rather than loving myself and using others, I now love God and give to others.

We see this at the start of the New Testament church in the book of Acts: 'All the believers were together and had everything in common. They sold property and possessions to give to anyone who had need' (Acts 2:44–45).

This was not an enforced commune-type living. It was a voluntary giving up of ownership for the sake of others.

This outward-looking generosity flows from the gospel. The gospel is about how God has been generous to us through Jesus. Paul explains the gospel in financial terms to the Corinthians: 'For you know the grace of our Lord Jesus Christ, that though he was rich, yet for your sake he became poor, so that you through his poverty might become rich' (2 Corinthians 8:9).

In spiritual terms, we've been made millionaires through Jesus. Jesus generously gave to us. And Paul then calls upon the Corinthian believers to follow that example and so to be generous. Our hearts are turned outwards, so that instead of selfishness, we rejoice in generosity. So that we earn, rather than steal, and then we give.

One of the great delights for me in church life is seeing people doing this. In our church recently, I have seen:

- someone lending a car freely;
- a group giving time and energy to transform someone's garden;
- a couple giving a work bonus to someone in need to pay for childcare;
- a gift of cash to a family to help them go on holiday.

And much, much more. Rather than taking from one another, the church is to be a place of giving.

Responding to God

Once again we may feel convicted of sin. That is one of the effects of God's law at work in the hands of the Holy Spirit. We may need to confess something to someone and apologize, as I had to do over my book 'borrowing'. We may need to change our practices at work or online. One of the most helpful things to do here is to call our actions what they are: say to yourself and others that you have stolen. Call yourself a thief! That names our sin for what it is and helps us take it seriously.

But probably most of all, we might have realized that we are very selfish. This has made me realize the ugliness of my own heart. We should hate the selfish self-orientation of sin shown in stealing, and long for the generous love of giving.

So once again, we run to Jesus and thank him for his forgiveness. We celebrate his generous giving of himself. And we ask that God would use that to transform our hearts.

9. SPEAKING TRUTH

I remember very clearly the experience of jury service. After hours of waiting around, I was finally part of a jury and hearing a case. The first witness was the man making the accusation, and he spoke about how the defendant had attacked him on the street for no good reason. I started to get angry on his behalf for this terrible action.

Then the defendant told a completely different story. Not just a variation on the first story, but one that took place in a different setting altogether, with a different sequence of events. He admitted hitting the guy, but explained how he was defending himself after this guy had tried to run him over.

What became very clear was that one of them, or both of them, were lying. And it wasn't just them. There were family members and friends who testified and supported their respective stories. It was outright, blatant lying under oath.

That was one example of lying. But there are so many others too. I reckon most news stories today involve the question of who is telling the truth and who is lying. It might be an accusation, the truth of a political agenda or an investigation into a hospital, but we wonder whom we can believe, because we know all too well that people lie. One of the greatest causes of our cynicism with politicians and other public figures is that we think people 'spin' the truth.

That is lying 'out there'. But then there are our personal experiences. The person who misled you over a purchase or a business deal. The workman who said he'd come back to fix the problem but never did. The friend who you later discover lied to you.

And then there are the lies that come from our own lips. They might not be as blatant, and they might not be under oath, but they are lies nonetheless.

We have all heard lies, been told lies and spoken lies ourselves.

The ninth commandment says, 'You shall not give false testimony against your neighbour' (Exodus 20:16).

Promoting justice

The first thing that this command is telling us to do is to promote justice. The 'testimony' referred to is what you would say in a court case. So this command begins in the legal world.

We must remember that this was before the age of fingerprints and DNA testing. Justice was established primarily, or even solely, on eyewitness testimony. Local leaders would investigate accusations by calling in witnesses. And God calls his people to speak truthfully and so to promote justice in their society, not to give false testimony which would lead to miscarriages of justice.

We can see this in some of the specific laws that flow from this commandment. Some of them repeat and expand on the command itself: 'Do not spread false reports. Do not help a guilty person by being a malicious witness' (Exodus 23:1).

This prohibits 'false reports' that would smear someone's name. It was very easy to spread a story around that wasn't true and so to damage someone's reputation. In particular, you are not to help a friend get off the hook by being a 'malicious' witness. That might mean lying to help them, or attacking the other party to help them. Don't do it.

God is also very aware of the power of peer pressure, so he adds, 'Do not follow the crowd in doing wrong. When you give testimony in a lawsuit, do not pervert justice by siding with the crowd' (Exodus 23:2). Don't say something untrue because everyone else is saying it. If you do, you will 'pervert justice'.

The book of Proverbs offers lots of reflections on this area:

A corrupt witness mocks at justice,
and the mouth of the wicked gulps down evil.
(Proverbs 19:28)

Like a club or a sword or a sharp arrow
is one who gives false testimony against a neighbour.
(Proverbs 25:18)

A truthful witness saves lives,
but a false witness is deceitful.
(Proverbs 14:25)

You can mock justice, hurt and damage people through telling lies, or you can honour justice, protect people and save lives through the truth.

An appalling example of this is seen later in Israel's history. King Ahab wants a vineyard belonging to his neighbour

Naboth, but Naboth won't sell it. So Ahab's wife Jezebel arranges for Naboth to be accused by two false witnesses of cursing God and the king. On the basis of their testimony, Naboth is killed (1 Kings 21:1–14). It's false testimony that results in death.

If someone did give false testimony to land someone else in trouble, then the Old Testament law had a very simple punishment: that person should receive the punishment for the crime he or she was accusing someone else of.

> If a malicious witness takes the stand to accuse someone of a crime, the two people involved in the dispute must stand in the presence of the LORD before the priests and the judges who are in office at the time. The judges must make a thorough investigation, and if the witness proves to be a liar, giving false testimony against a fellow Israelite, then do to the false witness as that witness intended to do to the other party.
> (Deuteronomy 19:16–19)

That is both a strong deterrent and fair punishment.

Concern for false testimony then flows out to justice more generally. For example, God's people are told:

> Do not deny justice to your poor people in their lawsuits. Have nothing to do with a false charge and do not put an innocent or honest person to death, for I will not acquit the guilty.
> Do not accept a bribe, for a bribe blinds those who see and twists the words of the innocent.
> (Exodus 23:6–8)

Here the concern is justice for the poor who can't easily defend themselves. This is connected to false charges and bribes that tempt us to change our testimony.

God is aware that we could show favouritism, and so injustice, in different directions, and so he warns against both: 'Do not pervert justice; do not show partiality to the poor or favouritism to the great, but judge your neighbour fairly' (Leviticus 19:15).

This also means that people had a responsibility to speak up if they knew something significant. Lying was not an option, but silence was not to be an option either: 'If anyone sins because they do not speak up when they hear a public charge to testify regarding something they have seen or learned about, they will be held responsible' (Leviticus 5:1).

When I spoke on this topic once, a teacher told me afterwards about a situation in the school where she worked. There had been an investigation over a serious issue by an outside agency. This woman hadn't been called to answer any questions herself, but felt that the truth had not come out, and so she put herself forward to say what she knew. We are to promote justice, and so silence is not an option.

These laws are there to promote justice, and so they show us both the rightness of justice and people's right to justice. Behind this is the fact that God is a God of justice. He only wants guilty people punished and he always wants innocent people protected.

So if we are ever a witness to an accident or a crime, we must speak the truth, the whole truth and nothing but the truth. Even if it involves friends or family members where we are tempted to slant what we say to protect them, we must not cover up or shift the blame.

This also means we have a concern for justice generally. God condemns favouritism, bribery and anything else that perverts the course of justice. And so we will want to promote that principle in our legal system.

We should also be grateful. In the UK, our legal system has all sorts of problems and issues, but overall it is based on this sort of concept of justice. And overall it works. Speaking to friends who live elsewhere in the world where bribery and corruption are normal, we realize we should be thankful.

Respect reputations

Second, although this command begins with false testimony in the law courts, it has wider application too. It calls us to respect reputations. When you give false testimony, you are giving evidence against someone. But you don't need to be in a law court for that to happen. You can say things about people over a coffee, at which point it is not 'perjury' (lying in court), but it is 'slander'. God has strong words about this too: 'Do not go about spreading slander among your people' (Leviticus 19:16).

> Whoever conceals hatred with lying lips
>   and spreads slander is a fool.
> (Proverbs 10:18)

When Jesus lists some of the Ten Commandments and expands on them, false testimony is widened to include 'slander' (Matthew 15:19). So Jesus thinks this command applies to saying untruths about people generally.

Just to be clear, slander is speaking falsely about someone, and we can also add libel, which is writing falsely about someone. What we say over a coffee or what we write on social media about other people can be very significant indeed. While it's not in a court, it is in front of, or to, other people. It doesn't affect a legal decision, but it does affect someone's reputation. It doesn't result in a legal verdict, but it does result in a communal verdict.

As with all sin, this comes from our hearts. Our heart can want to put people down rather than lift them up, and we can want to slur people's reputation rather than respect it.

In doing so, we are following the example of Satan. Satan told the first-ever lie in the Garden of Eden. He lied about God and did so to slur God's reputation. He tried to get Adam and Eve to think wrongly about God, and unfortunately they believed him. That shows us what an evil thing this is.

Slander then slides into the area of gossip – Paul includes it along with slander in a list of sins that break relationships (2 Corinthians 12:20). Gossip isn't the same as slander in that it is usually true, but it often involves a half-truth, an angle on the truth, or a truth that should remain private. In gossip, people are blamed for mistakes, their failings are exaggerated, and unfairly negative things are said about them.

We like gossip because it usually tarnishes someone's reputation. And our culture loves celebrity gossip because we can now look down on those we thought were above us. Proverbs speaks about our desire for tasty gossip:

> The words of a gossip are like choice morsels;
>> they go down to the inmost parts.
> (Proverbs 18:8)

And it speaks about the destructive results:

> A perverse person stirs up conflict,
>> and a gossip separates close friends.
> (Proverbs 16:28)

This means that when we hear gossip about someone, we should be both hesitant in believing it and quick to speak up for that person when we have reason to do so. We strive to respect and protect people's reputation. Which of course means not passing on gossip to others.

Integrity of speech

Third, this commandment is about integrity of speech more generally. God's people were simply told, 'Do not steal. Do not lie. Do not deceive one another' (Leviticus 19:11).

Here lying is linked with stealing and deceiving. It's the lie of the con artist or the false insurance salesperson. It is misleading people for your own gain. By contrast, God wants his people to be known for being trustworthy in their words.

Again, Proverbs speaks about lying generally:

> A lying tongue hates those it hurts,
>   and a flattering mouth works ruin.
> (Proverbs 26:28)

When we lie to people, we are hurting them and actually revealing that we hate them. Even if those lies are saying nice things – flattering them – it works ruin. This proverb comes in a section about misleading people or being a hypocrite where we say one thing but we do another. It is a matter of integrity that our words can be trusted.

This doesn't mean that we have to say everything we think all the time. That would be a disaster for me at least! We recognize that unpleasant and rubbish thoughts often pass through our heads and we should squash rather than speak them. Proverbs also tells us to guard what we say. The point here is simply this: when we do speak, people should be able to trust our words. Our speech should be marked by integrity.

We need to know that God feels strongly about this. We tend to think that lying isn't a big deal because it doesn't have the same obvious consequences as murder, adultery or theft. But listen to this:

> There are six things the LORD hates,
>   seven that are detestable to him:
>   haughty eyes,
>   a lying tongue,
>   hands that shed innocent blood,
>   a heart that devises wicked schemes,
>   feet that are quick to rush into evil,
>   a false witness who pours out lies
>   and a person who stirs up conflict in the community.
> (Proverbs 6:16–19)

So this is what God hates, what is detestable to him. And it includes lying lips and false witness. And they are put alongside murder and evil. Lying is a serious business.

Positively, we're told:

> The LORD detests lying lips,
>   but he delights in people who are trustworthy.
> (Proverbs 12:22)

> Kings take pleasure in honest lips;
>   they value the one who speaks what is right.
> (Proverbs 16:13)

> An honest answer
>   is like a kiss on the lips.
> (Proverbs 24:26)

We're to be people who can be trusted. Our integrity here is the link between our words and our character.

So Paul says, 'Do not lie to each other, since you have taken off your old self with its practices and have put on the new self, which is being renewed in knowledge in the image of its Creator' (Colossians 3:9–10).

We are not to lie because we are new people, people who are being renewed to be more like our Creator God. We have a new character, and lying is part of the old nature.

So we don't lie when we are tempted to cover over a mistake or to avoid having to confess a sin to someone. We avoid lying through exaggeration that easily becomes boasting to impress others. We resist the temptation to lie at work through promising better results than we can give, or through misrepresenting the opposition.

The result is that we will be known to be trustworthy.

Can I ever lie?

So can I ever lie? Let's think through some scenarios.

What about when I'm asked a question that I don't want to answer honestly. Unless we need to speak up to defend someone or establish the truth, there is no requirement to answer. In many cases, we can simply reply, 'I'd prefer not to say.' Or we can acknowledge an issue without having to divulge all the details. Someone recently asked me how I was, and I was tempted to say, 'Fine, thanks'. But it simply wasn't true, because I was wrestling with a complicated pastoral issue in our church. I didn't want to go into any detail with this person. So I said simply, 'There's some stuff going on that's worrying me, but I can't go into it.'

What about when a non-answer gives the game away or complicates things? It is so easy to lie in such situations. But I can't see that it is justified, and instead we should speak with integrity and trust God for the consequences.

Are there any exceptions? Yes, there are. Telling jokes, for example. No one thinks you are trying to tell the truth in a joke. Nor does anyone think you are trying to tell the truth when you're being ironic. What about lying for the sake of practical jokes? We need to be careful, but I think we have to judge what the cultural understanding is, that is, whether the people around us would consider it 'lying'. I don't mean that our culture sets the standard, but in some areas, like these, no one would think you were being deceptive.

But what about when telling the truth will have terrible consequences? The classic question on lying is what you would have done in the Second World War if you were hiding Jews, and the Nazis come knocking on your door. 'Are there any Jews here?' they would have asked. What do you say?

We need to acknowledge that Christians have varied in their responses. Some have said it is permissible, pointing to examples of lying in the Bible – like Rahab lying about hiding the Jewish spies (Joshua 2), and Jeremiah lying about his conversation with King Zedekiah (Jeremiah 38:24–27). These are sometimes seen as examples of lying to prevent terrible consequences like murder, and so when you know that's the case, then it is justified.

Others have responded that while those examples obviously exist, the people in question were never commended for lying. This group think lying is always wrong. That doesn't mean you have to reveal the truth; when the Nazis knock at the door, you simply say, 'I'm not going to help you in any way.'

Now, we should be aware that even if you think lying is OK in some situations like that, they are extreme situations indeed. Virtually all of them in Scripture involve avoiding death. If there is an argument for 'justified lying', it runs along these lines: because I know this person has an evil intention to harm someone, he or she has now lost the right to the truth, and so I am not obliged to give it. But that requires that I know the individual has such a murderous intent. In other words, this course of action cannot be used simply to avoid unpleasant consequences.

But can I lie to the Nazis? I have changed my mind on this – several times! Which I hope only shows that the arguments are finely balanced and it's hard to choose. Right now, I would say, 'No, I shouldn't lie.' However, wherever we land, we must recognize that this is an occasion that is going to be exceptionally rare for most of us.

This raises a broader question of how we make moral decisions. Do we choose the 'lesser of two evils'? Do we weigh the consequences of a decision and then choose the least-bad outcome? Am I justified in my 'lying' because a better result ensues?

Once we have said it's OK to choose the lesser of two evils, we could justify all sorts of things. For example, we could decide to lie about a sin to our spouse because we think the truth would hurt him or her too much. We could lie at work to protect our job because we need to provide for our family. And so on.

This leads to what's often called 'situational ethics' where you decide how to act on the merits of each situation. You judge the likely consequences or outcomes and then you decide which is the best, or the least worst.

We could have asked this question about any of the commandments, but it is most relevant to lying. Why? It's because we don't think lying is all that bad. We could have asked if murder or adultery were ever justified, but we'd all tend to say no, because we can't easily imagine a situation where they are. But with lying? We don't think it's such a big deal, so breaking the command for the sake of a better outcome almost seems wise.

Almost. But Jesus tells us that God's laws, including not lying, are the very ways in which we will love people. The law tells me what love looks like in practice. It tells me the best thing to do in every situation. So I will love my spouse by never lying to him or her.

The 'lesser of two evils' choice is usually actually a choice between a sin and an unpleasant outcome. They are not two 'evils' at all. If I think one of the choices involves sinning and the other doesn't, then my choice is clear, even if I don't like where that will lead.

To put it differently, God doesn't call us to judge the possible outcomes and then decide what's right. Of course, we are to be wise about outcomes and act accordingly, but not when it involves disobedience. God calls us to obey, and trust him for the consequences.

Responding to God

Once again we need honest confession. We need to own our sins of speech: lying, slander and gossip. We need to own them as sin, not just slips of the tongue. We need to recognize that God hates lying.

Then we look at Jesus. People attacked Jesus' reputation, they spoke false things about him, and at his trial people gave false testimony against him (Matthew 26:59–60).

But Jesus never told a lie. Peter says:

> He committed no sin,
>   and no deceit was found in his mouth.
> (1 Peter 2:22)

He obeyed where we have failed. And he died in our place to bring us forgiveness for every lie. Rejoice in that.

And then ask for God's help in that process of renewal. We have taken off the old self and put on the new; we are being renewed in God's image, and that includes renewal of our speech so that we are people of integrity whose words can be trusted, just like our God.

10. LIVING WITH CONTENTMENT

Do you ever suffer from food envy? You're eating out with friends or family. You've studied the menu and ordered your food. But when it arrives on the table, you instinctively look across at other people's plates and think, 'I want theirs.'

Why do we do that? Why do we do that before we've even tried our own dish?!

We too easily assume that we're losing out, that someone else has got it better than us, that the grass is greener on someone else's plate.

And what is true for food is true across life too: houses, cars, spouses, jobs, clothes and lifestyles. We can all too easily find someone about whose lot we instinctively say, 'I want theirs.'

God knows what we're like and he has something to say about it in the tenth commandment: 'You shall not covet your neighbour's house. You shall not covet your neighbour's wife, or his male or female servant, his ox or donkey, or anything that belongs to your neighbour' (Exodus 20:17).

Not coveting

Notice two things about this command. First, see how comprehensive it is. It pictures you looking over the fence at your neighbour and seeing his house. Then, within the house, the most obvious thing is his wife, followed by his servants. Then it moves to his most prized possessions, his best animals. And it finishes with 'anything that belongs to your neighbour'. It includes anything and everything that is his.

Second, notice the repetition of the ownership of these things. It is your *neighbour's* house, your *neighbour's* wife, *his* servants, *his* animals, or anything that is your *neighbour's*. It covers everything that is his, because it is his and not yours.

What are you not to do though?

You are not to *covet* these things. Coveting is a desire for ownership when something belongs to someone else. It is the look that doesn't simply say, 'That's nice', but, 'That's nice and I want it.' The first thought is appreciation; the second is coveting. When the Ten Commandments are repeated in Deuteronomy, Moses uses this same word, 'coveting', and then he adds another one in parallel with it: 'You shall not *set your desire* on your neighbour's house . . .' (Deuteronomy 5:21, italics mine). That's the idea of coveting: desiring for yourself.

Now, it is not that coveting is always bad or wrong. Not at all. The same word is used to tell us that God's commands are to be coveted or 'desired' more than gold (Psalm 19:10; see ESV). The question is whether the object in question is ours or not: we are not to covet what belongs to someone else. This command is saying that we are not to covet what is not legitimate for us to have.

This commandment is slightly different from the others in that it focuses on our hearts rather than our actions. It is only

slightly different though. As we've seen, behind the prohib-
ition of certain actions lie our heart attitudes, so the previous
commands have certainly involved our hearts. And as we will
see, flowing from this attitude will come a variety of actions,
so this command includes how we live.

Coveting in action

With the previous commands, we have been able to trace their
outworking through the detailed case laws for Israel. What 'not
stealing' looked like was unfolded in all the different situations
dealt with. But we have no similar unfolding for this command.
The reason is fairly obvious: what is being prohibited is
an attitude, and it is difficult to give precise case laws for an
attitude. Case laws work for concrete situations (what happens
when you borrow an ox); they don't work for hidden attitudes
(what happens when you desire your neighbour's barn).

We do see some examples in practice, though, later in
Israel's history. After entering the Promised Land, God had
said that the possessions from Jericho were all off-limits. But
a guy called Achan took some of them for himself and was
then discovered:

> Achan replied, 'It is true! I have sinned against the LORD, the God
> of Israel. This is what I have done: when I saw in the plunder a
> beautiful robe from Babylonia, two hundred shekels of silver
> and a bar of gold weighing fifty shekels, I coveted them and took
> them. They are hidden in the ground inside my tent, with the
> silver underneath.'
> (Joshua 7:20–21)

He saw these beautiful and valuable objects, and he 'coveted'
them so much that he 'took' them. He desired and took what

was not for him. So he broke the command, 'Do not steal', but before that he broke this command, 'Do not covet.'

A later example comes in the condemnation of God's people by Micah. He is particularly concerned about injustice taking place, motivated by covetousness:

> Woe to those who plan iniquity,
>   to those who plot evil on their beds!
> At morning's light they carry it out
>   because it is in their power to do it.
> They covet fields and seize them,
>   and houses, and take them.
> They defraud people of their homes,
>   they rob them of their inheritance.
> (Micah 2:1–2)

These people were plotting evil in the form of land grabbing and house stealing. But it was because they coveted those houses and lands. Illegitimate longing led to illegal taking.

In the New Testament, James tells us, 'You desire but do not have, so you kill. You covet but you cannot get what you want, so you quarrel and fight' (James 4:2). The words used here ('desire' and 'covet') can again be used positively or negatively, all depending upon what is being wanted. The point in James is that these people want something they should not have and that they cannot get. The result is quarrels and fighting among them.

So coveting in the heart leads to wrong living. It is coveting that will often drive stealing and adultery. It will often be the motivation that means we lie to gain something. It can result in quarrelling and falling out.

But again this command is more focused on that element of desire in the heart than on the actions that result. We are not to long for what isn't ours, even if that longing stays in the heart and never results in action. God is concerned about our hearts.

Greedy for more

Coveting is closely connected to the idea of greed, where we want more, even if we have no right to it. This too is condemned by the prophets. So Jeremiah says about the people of his day:

> From the least to the greatest,
>   all are greedy for gain;
> prophets and priests alike,
>   all practise deceit.
> (Jeremiah 6:13)

The greed here is about having more and having it through dishonesty – that's why it involves deceit.

Ezekiel condemns the same attitude:

> My people come to you, as they usually do, and sit before you
> to hear your words, but they do not put them into practice.
> Their mouths speak of love, but their hearts are greedy for
> unjust gain.
> (Ezekiel 33:31)

The frightening thing here is that the people are coming to hear God's Word, and are even saying the right things – 'their mouths speak of love'. But inside, their hearts are longing for what isn't theirs.

In the New Testament, we read regularly about the dangers of greed. Jesus says, 'Watch out! Be on your guard against all kinds of greed; life does not consist in an abundance of possessions' (Luke 12:15).

When we covet, we have misunderstood what life is about. We have defined it in terms of what we own and have. So more and better stuff means more and better life! But Jesus says that's not what life is about. As a result, we need to be on our guard against all forms of greed.

The apostle Paul tells us:

> Those who want to get rich fall into temptation and a trap and into many foolish and harmful desires that plunge people into ruin and destruction. For the love of money is a root of all kinds of evil. Some people, eager for money, have wandered from the faith and pierced themselves with many griefs.
> (1 Timothy 6:9–10)

Loving money and wanting more is not only wrong, it's dangerous. It results in people wandering from the faith – they become enamoured with money and drift from Jesus. It results in being pierced with all kinds of griefs – it's a form of financial self-harm.

This issue of greed is so important that it is a key criterion for leaders of God's people. When Moses is looking for men to help him lead Israel, one of the criteria is that they hate this sort of dishonest gain:

> But select capable men from all the people – men who fear God, trustworthy men who hate dishonest gain – and appoint them as officials over thousands, hundreds, fifties and tens.
> (Exodus 18:21)

We see exactly the same for those who are to be church leaders when Peter says,

> Be shepherds of God's flock that is under your care, watching over them – not because you must, but because you are willing, as God wants you to be; not pursuing dishonest gain, but eager to serve.
> (1 Peter 5:2)

Leaders are to be those whose desire is to serve willingly, not to get more. Their attitude should be to want to give rather than to get. The apostle Paul points out his example in this area to the Ephesian elders:

> I have not coveted anyone's silver or gold or clothing. You yourselves know that these hands of mine have supplied my own needs and the needs of my companions.
> (Acts 20:33–34)

Rather than longing for what he might get from the Ephesians, Paul worked in a day job so that he could provide for himself and others. He was a model of giving rather than getting.

So coveting and greed are significant; just wanting 'a little bit more' is not a harmless thing. They are wrong attitudes that can lead us into all sorts of sinful actions, and they are dangerous to us. It is important that our leaders are not infected by them.

But why is it so bad? What exactly is happening in coveting? There are two answers.

Coveting as doubting God

The first answer is 'vertical': it is what coveting means for our attitude to God.

When we covet, we desire to have that which is not ours, that which God has not given us. We are not content with what he has given, and we doubt his goodness to us.

We see this in the very first sin in the Garden of Eden. God had said that Adam and Eve could eat from any tree except one. There was one 'No' in a whole world of 'Yes'. But the serpent led Eve to want the one thing that was off-limits. The route to this was tempting her to doubt God's goodness to them and his wisdom in restricting them. The result was that she coveted:

> When the woman saw that the fruit of the tree was good for food
> and pleasing to the eye, and also desirable for gaining wisdom,
> she took some and ate it. She also gave some to her husband,
> who was with her, and he ate it.
> (Genesis 3:6)

The fruit was 'desirable', that is, it was to be 'coveted' (it's the same word). And indeed it was desirable, except God had said 'No'.

The fundamental question here was whether they would trust God and live within the limits he had given, or break the boundaries and reach for what was not theirs. Behind that was their view of God: was he mean-spirited or generous towards them? Would they be better off without him? When we covet, we doubt God and turn away from him.

If my children were to steal some money (which, I should probably say, they've never done), part of the reason would be the desire for what it could get them. But also coming into play would be their view of my wife and me as their parents. There would be a belief that we hadn't provided enough; they would be doubting our goodness and wisdom. And that is what Adam and Eve were doing with God.

Coveting is at the very heart of sin.

We doubt God and reach for that which he has said 'No' to. We fail to trust him and depend on him and think we should take matters into our own hands.

Martin Luther saw clearly that the issue at stake in being generous or in coveting was whether we trusted God or not:

A man is generous because he trusts God and never doubts that he will always have enough. In contrast, a man is covetous and anxious because he does not trust God. Now faith is the master workman and the motivating force behind the good works of generosity, just as it is in all the other commandments.[4]

Trusting in God leads to contentment with what we have, and it goes hand in hand with the ability to be generous. Conversely, doubting God leads to coveting, anxiety and the desire for more.

Coveting is a serious business because it reveals what we think of God.

Coveting as hating others

The second answer on the significance of coveting is 'horizontal': it is what coveting means for our attitude to other people.

We know that all the commands in the Old Testament can be summed up by the command to love, including coveting:

The commandments, 'You shall not commit adultery,' 'You shall not murder,' 'You shall not steal,' 'You shall not covet,' and whatever other command there may be, are summed up in this one command: 'Love your neighbour as yourself.'
(Romans 13:9)

Breaking all the commands then is a way in which we fail to love people, or we could say, it's a way in which we hate people. Of course, that's very clear with something like murder, adultery or theft. But the same is true of coveting. Coveting is 'hating people' rather than loving them. This is why elsewhere Paul says, 'Love . . . does not envy' (1 Corinthians 13:4).

How is that so?

When I covet, rather than wanting what is good for my neighbours, I want what they have. Rather than being pleased that they can enjoy their houses, their spouses or their servants, I want to have them instead. What they have becomes loot that I want to steal from them. Coveting sees those around me as enemies I want to take from, rather than friends I want to support. Envy sees people as competition to beat, rather than people I am glad for.

When I covet, I hate my neighbour rather than loving him or her.

This is why James said that coveting leads to quarrels and fights among us. Reflect on a quarrel and you will find someone wanting something but being frustrated.

Coveting then is a destroyer of relationships. You are not good friends with those whose lives you covet. Coveting erodes trust and goodwill; it undermines care and generosity. Show me a church full of coveting, and I will show you a church lacking in love.

Contentment counters coveting

What then is the answer to coveting? Contentment!

Rather than looking over the fence and wanting my neighbour's house or car or wife, I am to be content with my house, my car and my wife.

Paul says, 'Godliness with contentment is great gain' (1 Timothy 6:6). This is very true, and yet we are very slow to believe it. Contentment doesn't sound very appealing. It sounds like putting a good face on disappointment. It sounds like accepting less than I really want. But it's not true: contentment is a wonderful thing; it is *great* gain!

The writer to the Hebrews says,

> Keep your lives free from the love of money and be content with what you have, because God has said,
>
> > 'Never will I leave you;
> > never will I forsake you.'
>
> (Hebrews 13:5)

We need to tell ourselves that we don't need more and more money, and we can be content with what we have because God will never leave us. Our contentment is tied to our relationship with God and our trust that he will provide and care for us.

The apostle Paul is an example of exactly this attitude and trust in God. When he thanks the Philippian church for their gifts to him, he goes on to say this:

> I am not saying this because I am in need, for I have learned to be content whatever the circumstances. I know what it is to be in need, and I know what it is to have plenty. I have learned the secret of being content in any and every situation, whether well fed or hungry, whether living in plenty or in want. I can do all this through him who gives me strength.
> (Philippians 4:11–13)

Paul says he has learned contentment. He has been in situations of need and times when he has had plenty. He's not saying that he's unaware of the differences; he's not removed from reality. He has simply learned to be content in whatever reality he is in. It is a contentment that is independent of his circumstances. This 'learning' means we can't simply flick a switch and just be content. Our beliefs and attitudes run deep in us, so we need to learn how to be content. And that flows from our relationship with God and especially our trust in him.

Compare this to our culture today. Advertising makes happiness turn on possessions or goods. So buy this car, this insurance, this perfume, those clothes, and then life will be good. Advertising works to create discontentment and then offers to meet it.

So luxuries are packaged as necessities. Buy this new TV package, computer game or holiday – it's just what you need. A well-designed advert makes me think, 'Yes, I do need that.' Despite the fact that I didn't even know it existed just a minute ago.

This means we will need to fight the messages of a consumer world that tell us that we always need more. We will have to fight the adverts that tell us that life would be so much better with this or that item. We will need to beware of the shopping channels or brochures that offer us satisfaction with every purchase.

And we will need to develop deep within us a satisfaction and contentment with what God has given us, rather than a desire for what he hasn't.

Back in the third century a guy called Cyprian wrote to a friend of his called Donatus. He said this:

It is a bad world, Donatus, an incredibly bad world. But I have discovered in the midst of it a quiet and good people who have learned the great secret of life. They have found a joy and wisdom which is a thousand times better than any of the pleasures of our sinful life. They are despised and persecuted, but they care not. They are masters of their souls. They have overcome the world. These people, Donatus, are Christians . . . and I am one of them.

Contentment is a great mark that we are one of God's people.

Responding to God

We all covet. In fact, we probably covet more than we realize. The first thing we need to do is realize what we are doing. We are both doubting God and hating other people. Think about it in those terms. Think of the reaction of 'I want theirs' as an ugly thing.

Confess your sin. And then consider Jesus.

Jesus obeyed all the commandments perfectly. He never coveted. He never looked at someone else's life or possessions and wanted them for himself. Rather, he was glad for people. He obeyed this command where we fail, and he did so for us.

So we rejoice in Jesus' obedience of this command for us. And we look to follow in his footsteps, trusting God and loving people, and so being content with what we have.

CONCLUSION

I confessed to you at the start of this book that I wasn't keen on a sermon series on the Ten Commandments. I thought it would be predictable, negative and irrelevant. Maybe you had similar misgivings about this book? I hope that such concerns have long since gone – if you've read this far, then they probably have.

The Ten Commandments aren't predictable. I expect you've been surprised to see some of the ground we've covered and how far-ranging these commands are.

The Ten Commandments aren't negative. They actually hold up a wonderfully positive view of life at its best. If everyone lived out these commands, just think how different, and how wonderful, the world would be.

And the Ten Commandments certainly aren't irrelevant. They may have been framed for Israel thousands of years ago, but they reach into everyday life today. In fact, they reach into *all* of everyday life today.

When I preached that series of sermons, people commented more than once, 'God knew what he was doing, didn't he?' He certainly did. These are wonderful laws for life.

NOTES

1. A. C. Grayling, *The Good Book: A Secular Bible* (Bloomsbury, 2011).
2. http://www.iclnet.org/pub/resources/text/wittenberg/luther/catechism/cat-03.txt.
3. http://www.telegraph.co.uk/women/sex/divorce/7062152/Faithful-at-50-Dream-on.html.
4. Martin Luther, *Treatise on Good Works* 3, in Theodore Gerhardt Tapper (ed.), *Selected Writings of Martin Luther* (Fortress, 1967), p. 191.